ENDORS

T0163594

So many people are trapped in j̶o̶b̶s̶ ̶n̶o̶t̶ ̶o̶f̶ ̶t̶h̶e̶i̶r̶ choosing. Sri shows how by changing targeted destination – by charging forward on an entrepreneurial venture – one's inner passion and joy can surface.

BILL DIFFENDERFFER

Co-founder of Silvercar, former CEO Skybus Airlines, former CEO System One & author of *The Samurai Leader*

Sri takes the reader through an entrepreneurial journey – anyone trying to find purpose in life is blessed with concrete advice delivered creatively through multiple people with demonstrated success. It is hard not to be a winner if you implement the advice in the book.

RAO UNNAVA

Dean, UC Davis Graduate School of Management; Co-founder Angie's List

Most entrepreneurs, even the talented ones, fall short of their goals and fail. A few never get off the starting line, many stumble badly along the way. Destination Sucess informs and inspires readers to fulfill their entrepreneurial dreams with practical, proven advice. For those with aspirations to launch successful companies this easy to read book is mandatory.

THOMAS HARVAY

Senior lecturer, Fisher College of Business-The Ohio State University and former CEO AssurexGlobal

If you are an aspiring entrepreneur, or an existing business owner or leader who is looking to get more out of their life and business, Destination Success provides an insightful guidebook on your journey as told through the first hand experiences of super-successful entrepreneurs who pass on their wisdom for business fulfillment through this entertaining and fast paced book. In it you will learn valuable lessons about passion, people, purpose and profits that will fuel your dream and business growth!

RICK CROSSLAND

Founder of A Player Advantage and Author of *The A Player*

Reading Destination Success and the interactions with Sri on the valuable lessons taught in this book changed my whole purpose and vision for my business. It not only helped me double my business in the last 2-3 years, most importantly it helped me unleash my passion with purpose and set meaningful and achievable goals.

SANJAY THUMMA

Founder & CEO Vahrehvah.com Vahchef (You Tube)

DESTINATION SUCCESS

DESTINATION SUCCESS

Discovering the Entrepreneurial Journey

SRI GADDAM

NEW YORK

NASHVILLE • MELBOURNE • VANCOUVER

Destination Success

Discovering the Entrepreneurial Journey

© 2017 Sri Gaddam

Published in New York, New York, by Morgan James Publishing. Morgan James is a trademark of Morgan James, LLC. www.MorganJamesPublishing.com

The Morgan James Speakers Group can bring authors to your live event. For more information or to book an event visit The Morgan James Speakers Group at www.TheMorganJamesSpeakersGroup.com.

ISBN 9781683503873 paperback
ISBN 9781683503880 eBook
Library of Congress Control Number: 2016920350

Cover Design by:
Chris Treccani
www.3dogdesign.net

Interior Design by:
Chris Treccani
www.3dogdesign.net

In an effort to support local communities, raise awareness and funds, Morgan James Publishing donates a percentage of all book sales for the life of each book to Habitat for Humanity Peninsula and Greater Williamsburg.

Get involved today! Visit
www.MorganJamesBuilds.com

ACKNOWLEDGMENTS

I would like to thank the many people who have made this book possible:

To all my Harvard Owner/President Management Program (OPM 43) classmates for taking the time to share your real-life experiences and lessons with me.

A special thanks to Lilly Harris, CEO of Man-Machine Systems Assessment; Rohan Jetley, CEO of TGI Fridays India and Kiran Kancherla, CEO ERPAI for their enormous support and advice while completing this book.

To my mother Vajra Devi and father Srinivas Reddy for instilling values and the importance of education in me at a very young age. To my wife Chandana, son Yash, and daughter Mahita for all of their love, encouragement, and sacrifice throughout my entrepreneurial journey.

To all the members of the ERPA (ERP Analysts) family for all their support. Because of you, we have been able to build a wonderful company without compromising on our entrepreneurial spirit and rich values.

To the Morgan James Publishing family for your dedication to making this book be the best that it can be.

Finally, to my book architect Justin Spizman for his continued guidance, support, and knowledge which allowed me to bring this vision to life.

TABLE OF CONTENTS

FINDING YOUR PATH

*"There is no passion to be found playing small —
in settling for a life that is less than the one you are capable
of living."*
— **Nelson Mandela**

Do you ever feel like you have all the tools and qualities in place, but lack the drive, motivation, or even inspiration to succeed? You are not alone. We all experience a lack of passion at one time or another. Passion is the fuel that propels the car; without it, you are stuck, unable to move forward, and without a necessary energy source. This story is a true one, and it happens more than we'd like to admit. In fact, you'll likely feel a sense of familiarity with the forthcoming story. I would guess that is because we all have a little bit of John within us. In each of us resides a remarkable desire to succeed and feel happy about it in the process. But we then weigh that feeling against securing passion and purpose in our day-to-day lifestyle.

So, whom is this book written for? To start, this fable is told for anyone that wakes up, and heads to work wondering if there is more to life. Do you feel professionally unfulfilled? If you do, you are not alone. There is an army of people that look and act just like you. And if that describes you, then this story will be one of hope, if only to inspire you to survey your life, and make the necessary changes to elevate it.

Throughout this story, you'll learn real lessons from entrepreneurs who have crafted a lifestyle centered on purposeful work that is both satisfying and meaningful. These successful business owners and industry leaders have often lived through trial by fire, overcoming obstacles and challenges directly in their paths to become difference-makers and game-changers. You'll find that many of these business leaders attended extremely challenging business programs like the Owner/President Management Program (OPM) at Harvard, and used real life lessons to become trailblazers in their respective industries. The OPM program is a fantastic opportunity and welcomes successful business owners of all different shapes and sizes.

The collective knowledge of these exciting businessmen and women will serve as examples of people who have strived to create "trophy" lifestyles, and refuse to settle for anything but eternal happiness. After reading this book, you will find yourself in similar company. The experts interviewed and supporting stories will encourage valuable lessons that will help you to analyze your own life, evaluate your level of happiness, and if needed, begin a transformation to a better version of your current status.

Together, we can manifest great change in your life. Winston Churchill said, "Success is not final, failure is not fatal: it is the courage to continue that counts." Our story will be one of courage—the courage to take great risk to find great reward. With that said, I would like for you to meet my friend John.

CHAPTER 1

LESSON #1: THE QUEST:
Passion Leads the Charge

*"The two most important days in your life are the day you
are born and the day you find out why."*
— Mark Twain

John was smart, educated, and determined. No one would ever accuse him of lacking in ability or training. A graduate of Harvard Business School (HBS), John's teachers saw something special in him. It wasn't easy to stand out among his peers, but he did. There were no quantifiable reasons why exactly, but he was a magnetizing force, one that welcomed others and in fact, drew them in; once they entered his atmosphere, they were forever gripped. He was kind to his colleagues, caring, and always willing to take time to build relationships. He constantly volunteered, and tried hard to leave a positive mark on those with whom he had contact. So, it was surprising on many levels, to those that knew him and even to himself, that John awoke each day, struggled to get out of bed, and simply tolerated the day.

John was smart and different than his coworkers, but he was discontent with his current situation. He felt a bit lost, and needed guidance on where to go next. He knew he could find a life filled with purpose, one that made a difference in his life and in the lives of those with whom he worked — he just hadn't found that opportunity yet. But he was unwilling to give up, knowing that there was once a time in his life where he was fulfilled; where he was completely lost in the happiness of his career.

He often remembered his first full-time collegiate job, where he worked off-campus at a printing company, and quickly moved up in the ranks. During that first summer, he started as a presser, actually assembling the books. But within just a few months (and as the youngest employee by almost fifteen years), he was promoted to assistant manager of the store, where he was tasked with filling orders, reviewing final proofs, and leading a team of five people. The storeowner saw his promise, and quickly moved John up. But while John did a great job, he wasn't passionate about his work even back then. John had a way of getting lost in the responsibilities of the job, accomplishing and often exceeding goals, but still feeling unfulfilled in the process. On one hand, he was content with just being part of the process. But on the other, he knew he wasn't willing to take true risk and dislodge himself from the rat race of monotony.

*"Passion is one great force that unleashes creativity, because
if you're passionate about something, then you're more
willing to take risks."*
— Yo Yo Ma

It had to be his lack of passion. He didn't feel it, and so much of his averageness was directly associated to a lack of passion. At times, he wondered if he could pursue his dreams and make a difference in the world or create his own legacy that could be remembered for generations to come. He thought of his heroes, people like Steve Jobs, who were true innovators, and he marveled at how they let passion lead to enormous change. While his spark to light the world on fire was gone, John was often comforted knowing that there was a time in his life where passion burned wildly. Back at Harvard, he couldn't study enough. He couldn't pour in enough of his time and energy into his studies. He impressed his teachers, even overwhelmed them, with his thoughtful insight, unique thinking, and ability to solve extremely difficult problems.

He still remembers what Professor Smith told him at graduation: "John — you are something different. Your vision is brighter than the rest. Your heart beats stronger than your colleagues' hearts. Your soul is forged with greatness. Follow your passion and don't ever let your strongest attributes be lost in the mundane practices of a normal life."

And now here he sat, living the exact life that Professor Smith had warned him of. He had it all, but he felt he had nothing. Such is the case when passion does not lead the charge. A change had to be made. The credentials, the honors, and the awards meant nothing. Sure, his superiors viewed him as a potential all-star — he was on the rise. But he had no intention of ascending on this particular rocket ship.

So he awoke on that fateful day, and decided it was time to find the spark. He had to ignite the flame that would burn so deeply so as to light his heart and soul on fire. In short, he had to leave the practice of his mundane life and rekindle the flame that he so desperately lacked. Once again, it was time for passion to lead the charge.

Rekindling the flame sounded exciting. But John remained unsure where to begin. He knew his fire burned dimly, but where could he find the gasoline he so desperately needed? He once again thought back to his days at school, and reminisced about all the successful people he met throughout his life. He wondered what each of those people was now doing. He wished he could ask them questions like: Are you happy? Do you have passion within your life? How did you find professional and personal satisfaction?

Have you ever felt lost or disconnected? If so, how do you reconnect?

While he was sure he wasn't alone, John often felt like he was. He knew he needed to find the spark, the inspiration to go on, and create a better life for himself. He needed to find meaning within his own journey. He immediately thought the best way to do that would be to connect with <u>successful entrepreneurs</u> who had found meaning within their own professional lives. John knew where to start. As he sat in front of his computer, John pulled up the Alumnus portal for the Owner / President Management Program (OPM) at Harvard.

OPM is a unique program offered by Harvard Business School for successful business owners and entrepreneurs that lead companies with annual sales of at least $10 million.

He hadn't thought much about this as a resource, but he assumed it would be a good place to start. If he couldn't find anything there, he would move on to social and professional media options, like LinkedIn and Facebook, if necessary. He decided to first limit his search to those graduated within 100 miles of his current town. After a few clicks, the first result was for Srikanth Gaddam. Sri's profile on the Harvard Alumni Portal then appeared. It read:

> *Srikanth Gaddam is a seasoned entrepreneur who has launched four successful companies in the last 12 years, including ERP Analysts, Inc. Mr. Gaddam attended the Owner/President/Management program (OPM 43) offered by the Harvard Business School. He earned an MBA degree from the Max M. Fisher College of Business at the Ohio State University. He was a **Business First "Forty under 40" honoree** and 2015 **"Entrepreneurship and Innovation Award"** recipient from Fisher College of Business. He serves as President and CEO of ERP Analysts, a company that provides Oracle, Business Intelligence and Big Data consulting services, and delivers successful projects to mid-market and Fortune 500 firms.*

John was overcome by excitement as he processed the biography. He noticed a phone number and address for Sri, and without thinking twice, John crafted an email to Sri, introducing himself and congratulating him on the featured article. In his email, John explained he had a successful professional career, seemed like he had it all, and made quite a good living. However, even with all of this, he explained to Sri that he felt lost, unable to get unstuck, and dislodge himself from the quicksand that was aggressively encompassing his life. He shared with Sri that there was a time when it was all so easy, and happiness was around each and every corner. But at some point in time, John told Sri that he lost his drive, and the passion was gone. He explained to Sri that he wasn't exactly sure why he felt inclined to email Sri, but there was something about his story and his passionate approach to business that really connected with John. After explaining the purpose for the email, John shared with Sri he lived just an hour away from Sri and wondered if Sri would be willing to share a cup of coffee with him.

As John parked his car in front of Starbucks, he felt uneasy, as if he were about to enter a confessional, or maybe even an interrogation room. Either way, he was unsure what to expect, but knew he had to go through with it. He grabbed a table in the rear, a two-seater, with wooden, mismatched, hard-backed chairs. He ordered two coffees. He was excited when Sri responded to his email just hours later, and was willing to meet. As he looked towards the door, he saw Sri walk in, recognizing him from the color photo on the HBS alumni website. Sri wore a dark business suit, a checkered purple shirt, and black loafers. He surveyed the room, saw John wave in his direction, and moved toward him.

As they shook hands, John calmed down. Sri settled in the chair, and they shared the usual niceties but then jumped right in. John covered the last few years of his life, as well as his most recent job description. He explained to Sri most people would say John was crazy to feel the way he did. John had steadily progressed in his profession, owned a nice car and home, enjoyed a mid six-figure salary, and was constantly recognized for his performance and success in his position. But even then, it just didn't feel right. He ended his tale by sharing with Sri how he felt disconnected, disengaged, and disinterested in his current profession, even though it all seemed so perfect. Simply put, John said, "I lost my passion."

He then explained why he contacted Sri. He shared that he felt lost and was hoping that some mentorship could help to illuminate, maybe even ignite his own journey into starting his own business. John shared with Sri that he was captivated by Sri's journey, and recognized that Sri lived both a successful and meaningful life, personally and professionally.

Sri studied John, and digested all that he shared. He was sympathetic towards John, truly wanted to help, and understood how John felt, as it was common for many professionals to feel trapped and lost. Sri shifted towards John in his chair, and said, "You have really hit a dead end. It seems like you always had such a passion for your studies. I am so sorry you feel so unhappy in your life."

John exhaled deeply. "I know. It is a tough pill to swallow. The worst part is I really cannot even identify the moment when things truly went south. It was like a series of great misses that eventually led me to the destination where I stand today. So, I guess I am here to learn about you and your journey. I want to know what makes you feel satisfied. I want to learn what motivates you, what drives you to wake up each day, and live life with vigor and excitement. I want to understand how you recognized your passion. Can you share that with me?"

"Once something is a passion, the motivation is there."
— **Michael Schumacher**

Building Passion From Within

Sri paused and then smiled. "So, you want to know the secret sauce, do you? I haven't really thought about it in that way. It's not an equation, or a systematic series of steps, I guess. It's more like a way of being — a manner of existence. But I will tell you this: I've always made it a priority to focus on purposeful work, the type of thing that really motivates you to push forward, overcome obstacles, and wake up with an enormous desire to get the job done.

"I have actually dedicated myself to studying passion. It is a crucial aspect of our being, offering a sense of purpose, a feeling of fulfillment. It's not always easy to figure out your passion, but amazingly enough, I feel that passion is like a seed, already planted in your heart and soul. You are actually created with passion, like a default setting. All you have to do is find the sun and the water to nourish it so it can grow. And that is where many battles are fought.

Passion is really just a derivative of goal-setting. Meaning, if you set exciting goals, you'll want to achieve them at all costs. You will feel driven, dedicated, even determined to get to your target, through thick and thin. I have always felt that with passion, no obstacle is too big to stop you in your tracks. But without passion, any obstacle *can* stop you in your tracks. It really just becomes a mindset. But the mind is easily persuaded, and if you aren't excited about the goal, the mind will let you down. It won't move you to action, it will actually limit you from action. You have to choose your own goals, but if you don't wake up thinking about them and if they don't keep you up at night, they aren't big enough, and they aren't exciting enough. It should feel like a healthy obsession — like you are lusting after it. The more I talk it out, the more I realize that passion is just an ancillary effect of picking goals that really stimulate and enthuse you. If you do that, passion is easy."

He continued, "I know it's easy for me to say now, but it was not always so simple. In 1999, I was 25 years old and started my own business. I had a full-time job that lacked passion. And so I decided to quit, and I started a small company with the goal of hitting $1 million in sales in just two years. I had a great start and booked over $500K in sales in just the first six months, but our biggest customer was left bankrupt when the dot-com bubble burst. We then experienced great debt. That was an eye-opener, and it took us four years to recover and re-launch our operations. I quickly found out that success does not come easily, and you will likely fail, so get ready to learn from your mistakes. But you have to have a never give-up attitude and strongly believe you will achieve your goals no matter what the challenges. There was never a time where I stopped consciously thinking about my goal, and so I put my head down and started rebuilding my network and aligned it with my goal."

"The market eventually recovered, and I then decided to take the risk and keep pursuing my goal. In two years, I was able to successfully reach over $1 million in sales. After I reached my goal, I raised the bar and tried to attain $10 million in sales over the next four years. I realized you have to keep setting your goals, and we eventually became one of the fastest growing businesses in the United States. We now have over 500 employees and $75 million in sales. My next goal is to hit $100 million in sales over the next 2 years, and ultimately $1 billion by 2025.

"These may seem like unbelievable goals, but we were able to achieve these victories by systematically using goal setting principles. I think that is maybe where you should begin. To set goals, you have to really understand your need and your purpose. Remember, your need is where you identify the market need or a problem that is aligned with your passion and your purpose determines why it matters to you and others."

John squinted his eyes and nodded his head, as if to agree with everything Sri shared. He felt captivated by Sri's words, and it all started to make sense. He thoughtfully looked at Sri and responded, "That makes perfect sense. Pick goals that excite you to ensure your passion leads the charge. It is so simple. I guess I had never thought of it that way. I was always searching for passion, never realizing that it was just an ancillary result of meaningful and purposeful goals."

John took the small napkin from under his coffee and pulled out a blue ink pen from his pocket. He scribbled down the following equation:

Exciting Goals + Passion + Purposeful Action = Pinnacle or Destination Success

He pushed the napkin towards Sri, and Sri nodded his head. He said, "It makes perfect sense, doesn't it? If you want to be passionate, you have to:

1. *Set Exciting Goals*
2. *Unleash Passion for the Purpose*
3. *Take Purposeful Action*

"The goals help you to focus your energy, and then the action actually pushes you in the direction of fulfilling those goals. Passion is recognized as an ancillary result of those meaningful steps. Having said that, I guess the question remains: how can we each design a life filled with enormous passion? You should be proud that you have decided a change is necessary to your overall growth. Improving yourself is like giving yourself a second chance. I really love that you are not willing to listen to everyone else, as they would likely tell you that you should be happy where you stand. You have a good job, you make great money, and you are destined for success, at least by society's definition. But that is not always enough. Those who refuse to learn and improve will eventually burn out or be phased out. Lessons will always be learned in a hard and expensive way.

"So that brings us back to considering how we create exciting goals. That's what I want to leave you with. I have always thought that using the SMART goal structure is the best way to accomplish this. SMART is an acronym."

Sri took his own napkin and wrote down the following:

S — Specific
M — Measurable

A — Achievable
R — Relevant
T — Time-Bounded

"You must take action now that will move you towards your goals. Develop a sense of urgency in your life."
— **H. Jackson Brown, Jr.**

Sri then slid the napkin to John, and remarked, "You need to shift your thinking to consider how you are going to reach your goals. I feel strongly that you'll find passion if you create exciting goals. The best advice I can give you is to take the time to consider specific, measurable, actionable, relevant, and timely goals. If you do that, you'll find purpose, and you will feel as if you are constantly moving towards an exciting resolution. This is where I started, and I think it will serve you to do the same."

John responded, "Thanks so much. I really appreciate all of the guidance. I was told early in life that it is important to have mentors. I know it is pretty straightforward, but would you be willing to mentor me?"

Sri smiled.

"John, if you are willing to dedicate yourself to working on improving and finding your purpose, then I am willing to help you along the way. Let's go for it. I am sure we will learn a lot from one another."

"You got it, Sri. I will give this my all."

As John pulled into the driveway of his home, he felt inspired. Sri was kind, generous with his time, and left a lasting impression. John was motivated to grab a pen and paper and begin jotting down his own SMART goals. As he walked into his home, he greeted Charlie, his five-year-old Golden Retriever. Charlie was wagging his tail, hopping around the living room, and clearly excited to see his owner, as only a dog could be. John grabbed a legal notepad, cracked open a beer, and began to draw a chart. After a few minutes, John surveyed the large yellow pad, and felt satisfied with the following:

'SMART' Goals: SPECIFIC; MEASURABLE; ACHIEVABLE; RELEVANT; TIME-BOUNDED.
SPECIFIC: A specific goal is much easier to reach than a general one. Specific answers the what, where, and why?
MEASURABLE: What & how do you measure Key Performance Indicators (KPI's)?
ACHIEVABLE: Stretching and challenging goals that are achievable.

RELEVANT: Is it applicable in the current socio-economic environment?
TIME-BOUNDED (EXACT DATE): Goal without a timeline is merely a wish.

The easy part was done, but now John had to fill in the blanks. He exhaled deeply, and wondered how he was going to find meaning within his own journey. He promised himself that, no matter what, he would never live another day without taking action to reach his goals.

> *"The saddest people I've ever met in life are the ones who don't care deeply about anything at all. Passion and satisfaction go hand in hand, and without them, any happiness is only temporary, because there's nothing to make it last."*
> **— Nicholas Sparks**

John knew then it was time for passion to lead the charge...

Do you have exciting goals?

Are you taking regular action to move in the direction of those objectives?

Have you taken the time to focus your thoughts and behaviors to ensure you are inviting passion into your own life?

> *"The reason most people never reach their goals is that they don't define them, or even seriously consider them as believable or achievable. Winners can tell you where they are going, what they plan to do along the way, and who will be sharing the adventure with them."*
> **— Denis Waitley**

These are important questions to answer. If you aren't passionate, trust me that you are not alone. But like John, you can now implement strategies to focus your goals and invite passion into your life. Start with the SMART process outlined above. Grab a pen and actually fill in those blank boxes, to help you better understand where your passion resides. Only then can you ensure that you are ready to start taking meaningful action in the direction of exciting goals.

CHAPTER 2:

LESSON #2: FINDING MEANING WITHIN YOUR JOURNEY:

Purpose Beyond Profits

*"You were put on this earth to achieve your greatest self, to
live out your purpose, and to do it courageously."*
— Dr. Steve Maraboli

John left his meeting with Sri feeling rejuvenated. Inspired by Sri and his story, John decided that he would set a very specific goal: to create and build a company that was financially successful, purposeful, and worked to give back to the community. John desired to create purpose beyond profits, and wanted to ensure his business did the same.

It was a noble goal, one that many companies fell short of. John understood that you did not have to choose one over the other, and they could harmoniously exist in one company. John had a strong background in technology, and a simultaneous love for education and enlightenment, so he knew he'd have to find an intersection of these. But for now, he had to dig a little bit deeper into finding specific meaning within his own journey, so he could then project that purpose to the world.

> *"The heart of human excellence often begins to beat when*
> *you discover a pursuit that absorbs you, frees you, challenges*
> *you, or gives you a sense of meaning, joy, or passion."*
> **— Terry Orlick**

After taking a few days to consider John's new calling, as well as the exact path to achieve it, John decided to touch base with Sri, and bring him up to speed on his recent development. He picked up his cell phone, and called Sri.

"Sri...hey, it's John. How are you?"

Sri responded, "I am good John. How are things with you?"

"Overall, they are pretty good. Listen, I have really put a lot of time and energy into thinking about our conversation, and I cannot thank you enough for your guidance. In fact, I was even able to use the SMART process you outlined for me, and I came up with what I think to be a pretty good goal for the future. I determined that I want to get out of my comfort zone, and challenge myself to become an entrepreneur and start a business. I have not determined the product or service I plan to offer, but I did come up with a name for my business. I want to call it *Telos*, which is the Greek word for "purpose" or "goal." It feels right, and will always remind me exactly why I started this journey. My goal is to build a company that highlights and elevates purpose above profits, and offers the world something they need, not something they just want as consumers. I want my business to make its mark on the world and make it a better place. Additionally, I still need to find a few answers before completely filling out the SMART Goal process."

Sri paused for a second, as if to consider John's idea. He said, "I love it. You are really taking this seriously. If your goal is purpose over profits, then the word *Telos* is perfect for you. So, what are your next steps? Where do you plan to go from here?"

John sighed. "Sri, that is where I think I need your help. I have thought and thought and thought, and I cannot come up with anything specific to offer the world. Heck, I don't even know what sector I want to operate in. I feel overwhelmed and cannot find clarity in my journey. Any ideas on your end?"

Sri said, "That is a tough question to answer. I have found many entrepreneurs run into that roadblock. But the reality is that the best of the best have a calling, an inner fire that burns deeply and motivates them to create an avenue to spread that fire to the world. *It sounds like you have created a really thoughtful goal, but you have done it in reverse order, and it was intentional.* I wanted you to get started with a simple and easy-to- understand GOAL-setting exercise before digging deeper. Once you understand your ultimate purpose, you can easily complete your SMART goals. Now, you have to think of the offering that serves both purpose and profit. That I cannot answer for you. In fact, I don't think anyone can answer it. That has to come from within, but I am willing to bet it eventually will. It may not be today, or tomorrow, or a year from now. But I believe you will inevitably have that moment of illumination, when the light bulb goes off and you recognize exactly how you can help the world. However, maybe I can make an introduction that will help your light get a little brighter a little quicker.

"I think you should chat with Lilly Harris, a colleague and friend. President and CEO of Man-Machine Systems Assessment. She is a Government Contracting professional versed in all areas of business operations, business development, and the nuances of growing a family business. I really think she can help you find your direction. Lilly has worked extremely hard to make MSA a recognized leader within the community. She sits on a number of non-profit boards, volunteering for various charities, and loves to mentor young entrepreneurs like you. Everything she does, she does with purpose.

"You will love Lilly. Her business is a great example of how you can build a company that is not driven by profit, but by the desire to leave a positive impact on the communities that they serve. I am confident she can help draw out the best in you and inspire you to continue your journey. It's just not about profits for her — it's about legacy, it's about her people, and it's about leaving the world a better place. Why don't you give her a call?"

John excitedly said, "Thanks, Sri. That sounds amazing. Can you email me her contact info?"

"Of course," Sri said. "Headed your way now."

"In a world where there is so much to be done, I felt strongly impressed that there must be something for me to do."
— Dorthea Dix

John and Lilly exchanged emails, and eventually agreed to a meeting the next day at her office. As he was ushered into the conference room by the secretary, he saw Lilly sitting at the head of a large table, reviewing paperwork. John entered the room, and Lilly stood up, offered her hand, and then moved it in the direction of an open seat. John sat down, and thanked Lilly for her time. She then responded: "No problem. Sri gave me the heads' up you'd reach out. How can I help?"

John paused. "Well…I am not exactly sure where to start. Sri has been acting as a mentor of sorts, guiding me through a difficult time in my professional life. I make a good living in technology, I excel at my job, but I feel like there is more out there for me. I am not happy or satisfied. I feel like my job, and inevitably my life, lack substantial purpose. It is like I am doing everything right, but feel extremely uncomfortable in the process. I reached out to Sri on a whim, and he has already helped me tremendously. But we eventually got to speaking about purposeful business, and your name immediately came to mind."

Lilly said, "First off, let me tell you that I know exactly how you feel. I feel like we all get lost along the way, and it's not until we ask the big questions of life that we start to uncover our true selves. So this is a great start. Sri and I have had endless conversations about purpose and profit. He laughs at me at times because I always say that I would rather be purposefully poor than rich without reason.

"I was just going through the motions when I first started my career. I didn't have a clear direction of who I was or where I wanted to be in life. Like you, I had a great uneasiness that wouldn't go away. I felt as though many people feel like this at some point in their lives, but it's those who act on this uneasiness who change the course of their lives. For me, the uneasiness was unbearable. In response, I read books, I explored the world, I found people who were doing things I admired, and I then asked them to be my mentors. Once they agreed, I soaked in as much information as I could get. Throughout this journey I was able to start figuring out things that I wanted for my life. I would literally cut out quotations, pictures, to-do lists, and paste them on a poster board and look at them every day. Before I knew it, I was on-track to the life I wanted to live, a life beyond my wildest dreams. But I have to warn you, this process is fluid, and you must always be thinking ahead, tweaking as you go. I have a family now, and my needs have changed. What was once a self-serving vision of myself is now about legacy for my children and business.

"Once I found peace with my journey, I was able to be the best CEO for my business. The business then became a vehicle to help me manifest my dreams. I was able to design a business that would provide me the means to live the lifestyle I desired, offer stability for me and my family, satisfy my need to give back to my country, and to provide an environment where my team could thrive. But just as my journey has changed along the way, so has my business to meet my needs and the needs of my clients. Change can be scary, but it's necessary to grow."

John interjected, "I once heard a quotation: 'Don't follow money, the money will follow you.' I guess I never really realized it until I became entrenched in the workforce. I feel like most companies are just focused on profits. I want to build the kind of company that is focused on purpose, knowing that money will be an ancillary result of doing the right thing. But I still cannot get clear on what my purpose will be. I know I *want* to build a company that serves the community and makes a difference, but I just don't know how I can achieve that. It seems impossible."

Lilly quickly responded. "John — that is completely normal. You are not the first person with that issue. It is not something you just *do*. It is something you *are*. It is in your fabric, and it really cannot be manufactured, it has to be inspired, motivated, and produced."

"But where do I start?" John asked.

Lilly was happy to explore this with John, and continued on: "Let's focus on your purpose. What drives you, John? What makes you feel alive? Tell me more about who you are and what kind of leader you want to be. Once we start uncovering your true north, we can set up a business that will be in alignment with your talents and passions that can yield you enough profit for you to give back to the community and causes you care about."

John was eager to explore the notion that the business's purpose began with his own purpose. "So are you saying that my purpose in life and the purpose of the company are one and the same?"

"Well, sort of. Your company has purpose, because *you* have purpose. As the CEO, you can build your organization around your values, your mission, and your vision for the future. It's up to you to inspire people to want to hitch their wagon to yours. As a team, you can then amplify your efforts to do great things. You will attract like-minded people who will also want to be purpose-driven and give back. But it's your job to construct and nurture this within your organization. But let's keep it real — profits are necessary to do the things you want to do. You can't make a difference if you are out of business. For example, in my business we all subscribe to the notion that we can leave the world a better place by the services we provide. We seek opportunities where we can merge our talents and passion to serve our mission. For the past 25 years, this focus has allowed us to field technology that is worthy of our warriors and helps strengthen our national defense. This alignment keeps the team united and morale high. This is the glue that keeps us all together, but there is so much more to the business. We are focused on being relevant in the marketplace, providing cutting-edge solutions, closing new deals, customer service, making sure that our back office is in order, etc. These are the things necessary to remain in business. Don't take your eye off the everyday things that will build upon the legacy you are trying to create."

John was feeling a bit overwhelmed by all of this. "How do I figure out what my purpose is?" he asked.

Lilly said, "Let's start with asking yourself three simple questions:

1. *Throughout my life, what is a meaningful way I have worked to give back to those around me?*
2. *What do I believe in the most? Family? Education? Religion? Politics? Sports? Popular culture? It doesn't matter what you choose, but what topic keeps you motivated and inspired more than any other in your life?*
3. *If I could design the life I dreamed of, what would I be doing? And who surrounds me?*

> *"People who use time wisely spend it on activities that advance their overall purpose in life."*
> **— John C. Maxwell**

"I know, I know…it sounds so easy but, in actuality, is quite difficult. But I think you can start your journey by creating a mission for yourself. To this point, you have shared with me that you want to create a business that maintains great purpose, which helps others, and leaves the world a better place. That is a pretty clear and thoughtful goal. But that is where every business should start. Now we have to figure out how your purpose will help you to achieve that goal."

Lilly exhaled, and then said, "John — I do not know you well. But I sense that you care deeply about your life and the lives of others. That shows you are a purposeful individual. Otherwise, you wouldn't ask about my life and my business. So, don't beat yourself up, because there is something inside of you, an internal compass. These are tough questions to consider, but these three questions I outlined should help you on your journey. Just be patient, keep asking questions and seek out people who have created what you want and learn from them. If I can help you in any other way, don't hesitate to pick up the phone and reach out."

"Thank you Lilly. You have helped me more than you know. Your insight is helpful, and I am hopeful I can secure the same purpose and meaning in my business that you have in yours."

"I have no doubt you will," Lilly said warmly. "Talk to you soon."

John left Lilly's office, and exited the building onto the busy street. As he made his way towards his car, he was both excited and fearful he might never recognize the pathway to purpose. Even worse, he didn't know what his business could offer the world. His mind continued to wonder and his eyes eventually became heavy with all that he learned in just a few hours with Lilly. He drifted in and out of focus, and eventually found himself grinning from ear to ear, watching people pass by him to the left and to the right.

His new journey was already starting to pay dividends…

"I truly believe that everything that we do and everyone that we meet is put in our path for a purpose. There are no accidents; we're all teachers — if we're willing to pay attention to the lessons we learn, trust our positive instincts and not be afraid to take risks or wait for some miracle to come knocking at our door."
— Maria Grubbs

John reflected on his meeting with Lilly. It was inspiring to meet someone that was both grounded and successful. She never fought the battle between purpose and profit, but rather, worked to ensure the two were harmonious within her business. John was half-inspired and half-jealous, wishing that he had secured that same balance. But one thing Lilly said, more than anything else, remained with John: *Lilly shared with John that purpose was in his subconscious. Meaning, it was inside of him, he just had to find it.* He felt that way, but it sure was comforting to hear it from someone else. So with that said, John took out his journal and began to answer the questions posed to him from Lilly. After close to an hour of writing, he put down his pen and took survey of his responses. They all seemed to pour out of his heart, and flowed easily onto paper. This felt reassuring, as if he were destined for these responses. John took a highlighter, and began to shade the common responses, the words that seemed to fit together. He then focused his attention on just the highlighted areas, to determine how they all fit. After a few minutes, he wrote down the following statement:

The intention of my journey is to find purpose and profits, through offering the world a technology that helps to link resources and education to those segments of society that lack these essential and fundamental means. I plan to be a leading thinker in bridging the gap between those that can and cannot receive the institution of schooling that every child should receive as a basic right of existence.

SMART GOAL: "Positive impact on 1 million children (Specific) by offering a technology that helps bridge the gap in the current education system (Relevant) with over $10M (Measurable) in sales in the next five years (Time-Bounded). This is definitely achievable."

"The meaning of life is to find your gift. The purpose of life is to give it away."
— Pablo Picasso

John read and reread this statement. He felt a sense of pride, and he truly identified with those words he placed on paper.

"Finally," John said aloud, "I feel like I have found my purpose and SMART Goal."

CHAPTER 3:

LESSON #3: THE LAW OF ATTRACTION:

Visualize, Believe, & then Achieve

"All that we are is a result of what we have thought."
— Buddha

J ohn picked up the phone and dialed Sri's number. Sri picked up after three quick rings.

"Hey John," he warmly said. "How'd it go with Lilly?"

John responded, "It went extremely well. She has remarkable amounts of passion, and it shows in everything she does. Our conversation was really inspiring, and I left feeling motivated to really figure this whole thing out. She provided me with some helpful guidelines, and, at the end of the call, I felt substantial clarity on exactly how I can find something I am passionate about. I used to think passion was a journey…something I was looking for. Lilly helped me to shift that vantage point, and I now realize that passion is not a destination — it is actually a calling. It is something within, something that is embedded and likely connected to our existence. I was passionate about my goals all along; I just did not realize where it was hiding. Lilly helped me to reach that conclusion, and then gave me some crucial steps to put my passion on paper.

"After our call, I actually was able to come up with the following intention that underlies my journey. Can I share it with you?"

"I would love to hear it, John," Sri stated.

"Great. The intention of my journey is to find purpose and profits, through offering the world a technology that helps to link resources and education to those segments of society that lack these essential and fundamental means. I plan to be a leading thinker in bridging the gap between those that can and cannot receive the institution of schooling that every child should receive as a basic right of existence.

"It really sounds better every time I say it. I have always enjoyed my educational journey. I feel connected to it, and want to help build a world that has the same love of education that I do. Growing up, I have always felt conflicted. I am lucky enough to have had every opportunity to learn. I understand I am the exception and not the norm. I did a little bit of research and quickly found some staggering statistics regarding education in both America and the rest of the world. It actually frightens me how unavailable a good education is to millions of children throughout the world. That should not be the case. Everyone should have access to opportunity. To that end, I want to bridge the gap between those young men and women that come from means, and those that do not.

"Sadly, I think that, as we progress, we will regress. The educational gap will likely widen, and if we don't do something soon, it will only get worse. So I wanted my destination to be purposeful, and directed toward being part of the change the world desperately needs. Which now, leads me to the next obstacle, which is to figure out exactly how I can accomplish this goal. It feels big, and I know that big goals call for big efforts. I guess what I am saying is that once again, I feel stuck. I do not know where to go from here."

"Take the first step in faith. You don't have to see the whole staircase. Just take the first step."
— Dr. Martin Luther King Jr.

Sri responded: "John, have you ever heard of the Law of Attraction?"

"I have. It feels a little touchy-feely, but I am open to your suggestions. What do you think about it?" John replied.

"The Law of Attraction is extremely basic, but it is very powerful. It is consistent with the notion that 'like attracts like,' and I firmly believe in it. If you have positive thoughts, you'll likely attract positive people. But if you constantly doubt yourself, and openly project negative thoughts, the world will give you poor results. But it is not just related to your thoughts; I think it absolutely applies to people and outcomes. Expound positive, and positive people will find themselves attracted to you. What you now need is to project positive vibes to the world, to see what the world gives you in return. You might just find that the people or the outcomes that come your way end up being exactly the light you need.

"For instance, Gaurav Bhalla, also a good friend of mine from HBS, runs one of the largest real estate development companies in North India, Vatika Group. Its portfolio includes companies from the food and beverage industry. Gaurav was obsessed with a new concept Nukkadhwala, which translates to "Corner Shop" in English. His concept was to establish your neighborhood local pit stop, serving authentic local food items from various parts of India. The Indian food and beverage market had never seen this combination of traits before. By definition, being obsessed means a relentless pursuit of something which escapes rationale. Gaurav is now operating ten outlets with a dedicated customer base in each one and showcasing great financial results. He is planning to open around 200 restaurants by 2020. His tenacity and focus on his initial vision with a positive mental attitude was the only path to create this distinctive concept. Today, he executes this with complete faith and a burning desire.

"My favorite book on the subject, Napoleon Hill's <u>Think and Grow Rich</u>, really offers an amazing study in this basic premise. I actually published an article recently, which covered and summarized the book, and its relationship with the Law of Attraction. Why don't you allow me to send you it, and you can review it on your own. I think it will really help you to gain insight into this extremely important message."

John responded, "That sounds like a great plan, Sri — please send it over."

"No problem. After you read the article, I would strongly recommend that you reach out to a good friend of mine and a classmate from HBS: Mike Podrazhansky, who strongly believes and practices the Law of Attraction."

John poured himself a large cup of coffee, sat comfortably on his oversized living room couch, and pulled up the email from Sri. Attached to the email was a document, entitled, *"Attainment of the*

Law of Attraction. " He downloaded the link, and his Microsoft Word program popped up, generating a typewritten file. It read:

Think and Grow Rich: A Summary of the Law of Attraction
By Sri Gaddam

Think and Grow Rich is one of the most celebrated, and often, recommended books on the topic of self-help and business development. Andrew Carnegie commissioned this book, and it includes interviews of 500 of the greatest men of the early 20th century, including Henry Ford, J.P. Morgan, John D. Rockefeller, Alexander Graham Bell, Thomas Edison, Theodore Roosevelt, Wilbur Wright, and W. Howard Taft. First published in 1937, it has now sold more than 70 million copies, giving it the distinction of being the all-time bestseller in the personal success category.

I certainly don't agree with everything in this book, but it stands to reason that uncommon success must come from uncommon thoughts and actions. If some of this advice seems a little "out there," or too intangible, vague and short-lived to be useful, remember who it's coming from, and suspend judgment until you've tested it for yourself. But, I feel like there is a strong connection to many of the building blocks discussed in Hill's book and the concept of attraction in general. After my review and detailed reading of the work, here are the top ten concepts that directly relate to The Law of Attraction:

1. Desire: The Starting Point of All Achievement
It may be stating the obvious, but growing rich starts with the desire to do so. The desire discussed here is not simply wishing, but is an intense, burning obsession, which must be coupled with both a plan

and persistence in sticking to the plan. The author presents a six-part method to ensure that this is the type of desire you are starting with:

1. Fix in your mind the exact amount of money you desire.
2. Determine exactly what you intend to give for this money.
3. Establish a definite date by which you intend to acquire this money.
4. Create a definite plan to acquire the money, and take the first step immediately.
5. Put the four items above into a clear, concise sentence describing each part.
6. Read the statement aloud twice daily, in the morning and at night.

The principle here is that desire has ways to "transmute" (transform) into its physical equivalent. This is the beginning of the key principle of the book: that the subconscious mind acts beneath the surface to accomplish what it is directed to accomplish. This is also the premise for an idea like the Law of Attraction. You have to visualize that which you want to achieve.

2. Faith: Visualization of, and Belief in Attainment of Desire

Of course, the subconscious mind must believe that something is possible in order to act on it. Faith is an interesting concept, but in this context the author defines it as "a state of mind which may be induced, or created, by affirmation or repeated instructions to the subconscious mind. It is by this practice that you can convince your subconscious mind to "translate that impulse into its physical equivalent, by the most practical procedure available."

The author attributes both good and ill fortune to this practice. In other words, someone who lets himself believe negative things has communicated to his subconscious to act upon those negative beliefs and translate them into reality. Someone who neglects this practice, and allows his subconscious to go where it will, risks being set up for failure by the operation of the subconscious that will continue regardless.

3. Autosuggestion: *The Medium for Influencing the Subconscious Mind*

The author asserts that exercising this control requires both conscious attention, and the mixing of emotion (a word the author uses interchangeably with "belief" or "faith") with what you tell yourself. He presents repetitive visualization as the best method of accomplishing this mixture — actually picturing the appearance of a specific amount of money, consistently over time. Eventually, this will cue your subconscious to "hand over" specific plans to begin to make it happen. Simply put, autosuggestion is the practice of communicating to yourself using your conscious mind for the purpose of convincing your subconscious. As humans, we can exercise complete control over what reaches our subconscious mind (through our five senses), but most people don't often exercise that control.

4. Specialized Knowledge: *Personal Experiences or Observations*

In this chapter, the author makes a down-to-earth assertion — that general knowledge itself is useless in accumulating wealth. You must have specific knowledge and skills (how to fix a leaky faucet, diagnose a disease, build a financial model, etc.) in order to add value and be paid for it. While this is a commonly misunderstood principle, it should be evident to anyone that general education does not correlate with wealth; instead, specific knowledge applied to specific tasks is what actually leads to money. That is, the Law of Attraction requires that you take active steps to position yourself for success.

5. Imagination: The Workshop of the Mind

Mr. Hill separates imagination into two conceptual types: synthetic imagination, which simply rearranges existing ideas into new concepts, and creative imagination, which creates something from nothing. Transforming desire into money requires specific plans, which come most often through synthetic imagination. The author scoffs at the idea that riches come from hard work; more often, he contends, riches of great quantity have come "in response to definite demands, based upon the application of definite principles... when a creator of ideas and a seller of ideas got together and worked in harmony." The ideas that come from imagination are the forces that cause things to come into being. You must add imagination to specialized knowledge to grow rich.

6. Organized Planning: The Crystallization of Desire Into Action

This next step toward riches requires an alliance with a group of people for the purpose of carrying out your plans. To succeed, you must be sure to compensate these individuals in some manner, meet with them at least twice a week, and maintain harmony with each individual in the group. Faultless plans are essential for the growing of riches, and only the abilities and imaginations of multiple individuals will allow the creation of plans that are perfect, or as near so as possible. Process of planning must be continuous and persistent, since failure will often come before success despite your best efforts. You must select individuals who are likewise persistent. In addition, you must develop the qualities of a leader if you expect to lead such individuals in any endeavor. That said, this principle plays in perfect harmony with the Law of Attraction, as it requires you to begin the process of planning your ultimate goals in order to better reach them.

7. Decision: *The Mastery of Procrastination*

The lacking of an ability to actually make a decision often separates those that reach the pinnacle of success and those that do not. Hill claims that without exception, all successful people have the habit of making decisions promptly, and of changing them slowly. People who have no desire of their own are heavily influenced by the opinions of others, and are not likely to succeed. Great accomplishments come from courageous decisions. The ability to decide quickly comes from knowing what it is you want, and it is that ability that defines leaders. As the author states, "The world has the habit of making room for the man whose words and actions show that he knows where he is going." The Law of Attraction requires that you consider what you want…and then act on it. Thought without action keeps you at the starting gate.

8. Persistence: *The Sustained Effort Necessary to Induce Faith*

The addition of willpower to desire is the basis of persistence, which must be applied to the other principles in this book in order to grow rich. Persistence is a state of mind that can be cultivated by having definiteness of purpose, desire, self-reliance, definiteness of plans, accurate knowledge, cooperation, willpower, and habit. It is often easy to actually say what you want — it becomes much more difficult to then maintain that belief system and persistence when the going gets tough. To attract anything into your life, you have to continue to focus on it, hold a deeply felt faith, and preserve it even during times of great challenge.

9. *Power of the Master Mind: The Driving Force*

The Law of Attraction requires that you surround yourself with same-minded people. In this chapter, Mr. Hill delves further into the necessity and power of the master mind, discussing both the economic and "psychic" features of having such a group of individuals to support you. The economic is simple; as discussed earlier, the combination of experience and brainpower is a serious economic advantage. However, despite the pages devoted to discussing the psychic feature of the mastermind, that particular component is more difficult to pin down.

10. *The Subconscious Mind: The Connecting Link*

Specifically addressing the central subject of this book, the author reminds us that directing the subconscious mind via the other principles discussed throughout this book is something that can be done only through habit. To grow rich, you must continually draw upon the positive emotions, rather than allow your mind to dwell on the negative ones. Faith cannot coexist with fear. This is a fundamental principle that controls the Law of Attraction. You have to plant the seeds of positivity into your inner-being, so that you actually default to what you want in a subconscious manner.

> *"You create your own universe as you go along."*
> **— Winston Churchill**

John closed his laptop, stretched his arms and legs, and began to reflect on Sri's article. He read Napoleon Hill's work twice in business school, but never quite knew what to think of it. The information was extremely detailed and, at times, tough to fully digest. But Sri did a wonderful job of focusing on its relationship with a concept familiar to most — the Law of Attraction. From that perspective, it made perfect sense. John now recognized that the Law of Attraction appeared in many forms, not just in the basic premise most of us know quite well.

John was more curious than ever to reach out to Mike and learn about how he practices the Law of Attraction. John scheduled an appointment with Mike and agreed to meet him in Atlanta in person.

Mike's schedule was booked solid, so John agreed to meet him at an airport restaurant as he was flying out of the country. The two coordinated to meet at Mulligan's, a large restaurant located in the International Terminal. When John landed, they exchanged texts and John found the restaurant, nestled in a busy corner of the Hartsfield-Jackson International Airport. He walked in, and looked around the restaurant. Eventually, he saw Mike waving in his direction. He moved briskly through the restaurant and made it to the table.

"Mike — it is so great to meet you. Thank you so much for finding time to meet with me."

"John, no problem at all. I am so happy we could find time to connect. Sorry this meeting is a little non-traditional, but it was the best I could do on such short notice."

John quickly responded, "That's no problem at all. I really appreciate your willingness to make it work. Sri told me a lot about you. Funnily enough, we were talking about the Law of Attraction, and he shared with me that you of all people attribute much of your success to this principle."

"Very much so. My story is one that I am very proud of. It just always seemed like I was in the right place at the right time, until I learned of the Law of Attraction. My parents were very poor immigrants. However, I was passionate about computers while growing up, and bought my first one in the early eighties when I was in elementary school. So, I just started writing programs as a little kid. I read all that I could to learn about software design. While growing up, I would visualize that I will make a great product, and that I am something special. I was a sponge, soaking it all in. I loved to read and write, and I worked hard to build a strong network of friends who were enthusiastic about computers and software design as well. Even as a child, I knew my true calling was in software design. I always maintained a faith in achieving my dreams and constantly worked with a positive mindset and a burning desire. I wanted to use that to make a positive impact on the world.

"When I turned 16, I took my first job at a local Kroger. I bagged groceries, and had a front row seat to the problems and inefficiencies of checking out. I noticed the lines were long and barely move. I wanted to find a solution. So I was determined to develop software to handle problems that the grocery store often faced, like Efficient Employee Scheduling, Reporting, and Management Software, which would help reduce the wait time and check out process at grocery stores. I hit the ground running, and after only a few months, I had a product I thought could make it a difference. I pitched it to my manager, and it made its way up the food chain. Eventually, Kroger purchased the software, and it helped them to substantially reduce payroll costs, and was the perfect fit between employees and their workload.

"That was really the first time I realized I could take my love for software design and use it to make money. So, I guess it was then that I started my first software design company. My burning desire and preparation landed me an opportunity to pursue my lifelong goal of creating software that would make a huge positive impact. My small software company eventually grew. I would always hear myself saying, 'Success is the intersection of preparation and opportunity.' I believe that if you strongly think and believe good things will happen, they are most likely to happen. So, in 2007, I sold my company and started another venture in the software field.

"This deal pretty much set me up to do whatever I wanted, but I decide to take some time and reflect on how I got to where I was in life. In hindsight, I realized that I would regularly do five things:

1. Think, believe, and visualize the result of my goal every day.
2. Be passionate about my goal.
3. Work hard to achieve my goal with a burning desire and positive mental attitude.
4. Never give up that attitude.
5. Always remain open to listening to new ideas.

"It was really those five rules that pushed me to reach my goals. I suppose they all are directly related to the law of attraction, in one capacity or another."

As Mike finished this statement, the loudspeaker came alive. John heard the announcement: "Now boarding, Delta Flight 152 to Munich, Germany."

Mike looked up at John and said, "Well, that is me. But I hate to cut this short. Let me give you my personal cell phone. Please use it if you need anything else. I would be more than happy to give you any information you may need."

John said, "Thank you so much for finding some time for me. I really enjoyed learning more about you. This was extremely helpful."

Mike packed up his bags, grabbed his carry-on, and exited the restaurant, heading in the direction of security. John looked at his watch, and noticed he had an hour until his flight home. He decided to take out his journal and jot down some notes.

"We are what we repeatedly do. Excellence, then, is not an act, but a habit."
— Aristotle

In that moment, John began to compartmentalize the law, and recognize how it spanned his own life, and how regularly it impacted his success (or lack thereof). He then began to review Sri's article, and take detailed notes, transforming Hill's words to Mike's interpretation, to John's own understanding and application of the rules of the road. He then took out his journal and wrote down the following:

People attract positive results and exciting people through three very important qualities:

1.   *The Right Attitude*
2.   *The Right Energy*
3.   *The Right Opportunities*

People create the outcomes they want when they approach life with the right type of attitude, i.e.a positive mental attitude. That means that they understand how they project to the world. No one likes a naysayer or a Debbie Downer, but they do appreciate perspective. People want to be around others that elevate them, and that uplift the overall way they feel about themselves. Do that, and people will covet your time, thirsting to be around you. Nothing is impossible to achieve in this world, one has to think and believe that he can achieve, and visualize the result and pursue with a burning desire.

Outcomes are also connected to energy. Energy is a quantifiable resource, and people choose to use energy in plenty of different ways. We waste energy on things with little value, and often times we make mountains out of molehills. If you want to attract the Law of Attraction, you have to use this precious and limited resource to your advantage. The right energy helps others, helps yourself, and is directly connected to the world as a whole.

Finally, the Law of Attraction is not based entirely on sitting around and visualizing an outcome. You have to put yourself in the position with proper preparation and a burning desire to succeed. There are way too many people that expect outcomes without taking advantage of opportunities. Networking events, introductions, lunch or dinner meetings, job fairs — there are too many in nature to name that are aligned with your ultimate goal. Be specific and precise with what you want, but the constant is that successful people seek out and seize right opportunities.

John ran through the rest of his notes, and could not believe the amount of information gifted to him during the course of the past weekend. He knew it would help him along the way. It was in that moment that John decided to create a workbook of sorts, like a map anyone could use along their journey. John knew this simple process could help him, and he felt confident it could help some of his friends and colleagues overcome some of the obstacles in their own path.

"There are only two ways to live your life. One is as though nothing is a miracle. The other is as if everything is."
— Albert Einstein

He started sketching out a page to summarize his game plan to outline the Law of Attraction. It looked like this:

Finding the Law of Attraction

1. Write down my ultimate goal with a definite date.
2. I will have complete faith that I will achieve my goal without any doubt.
3. I will read the statement aloud twice daily — in the morning and at night, and visualize the result to influence my subconscious mind.
4. I will make a habit of making decisions promptly, and of changing them slowly.
5. I will put together a Master Mind Alliance, who are aligned with my goal and help me to execute it successfully.
6. I will continually draw upon the positive emotions, rather than allow my mind to dwell on the negative ones without fear of losing.

"Remember, happiness doesn't depend upon who you are or what you have, it depends solely upon what you think."
— Dale Carnegie

John reviewed his notes and decided he would recite these on a daily basis. It would take a few minutes each day, but John recognized this process would not only push him to evaluate and then analyze those actions he takes on a daily basis, but also hold him to a higher standard, because he knew he'd have to answer to this questionnaire each and every day.

John felt relieved, as if he discovered an old friend, one that had given him so much, but one that he lost touch with over the years. He was excited to reconnect, and felt invigorated that Sri helped him to understand such an important work like Hill's <u>Think and Grow</u>

<u>Rich</u>. He was determined to share this with everyone, and take these powerful concepts and make them his own.

CHAPTER 4:

LESSON #4: CORE VALUES:

What are you Made of?

"When your values are clear to you, making decisions becomes easier."
— Roy Disney

ohn awoke early the next morning, and felt overcome by a sense of satisfaction. He knew he made tremendous strides over the past few weeks, and he knew he stood on the doorstep of great opportunity. He was clear on his goals and purpose, and felt he had the necessary tools to at least begin to shift his attitude to a positive outlook focused on building his business. However, even with all of the excitement of the last few weeks, he knew there was still one gigantic step he had to take.

John started to panic as he knocked on Tom's office door. He had grown to really like his boss, and they had built a pretty solid friendship, as far as boss and employee go.

He could hear Tom's booming voice say, "John — come on in."

As John sat down in the oversized chair directly across from Tom, his palms began to sweat. He felt nervous, warm, and was about to have a panic attack. He took three big breaths and started in.

When he was done, he looked over at Tom, who leaned back in his chair, and had a large smile on his face.

Tom said, "John, I didn't realize you were unhappy here. And boy, did I have big things in store for you. You have matured, grown, and shown an undeniable ability to lead. However, I am guessing those same qualities that I love about you are the ones that are pushing you to go and follow your heart. I could tell you any number of things and try and persuade you to stay, but I know that would be a waste of your time. But I will tell you very directly: if you do not know what you are made of….then the next few years are going to really answer that question for you."

> "Be more concerned with your character than your reputation, because your character is what you really are, while your reputation is merely what others think you are."
> — **John Wooden**

John thanked Tom for all he had done, gave him a big hug, and indicated that he would be more than willing to remain in his current position for a few weeks, or at least until Tom could locate a replacement. Tom politely declined, and jokingly told him he didn't want anyone in his office that wanted to be somewhere else. John understood his position, and went back to his office to pack his items. He could only manage to fill one small box with his personal effects, but, in that moment, he felt the weight of the world was removed from his shoulders.

Now, all he had to do was to figure out how to start a business, and generate sufficient income to actually pay all of his bills. Regardless, he felt strongly that the most difficult part of his journey was behind him. As he walked out of his office building for what he thought would be the last time, he considered a question Tom left floating around in his mind: *What am I made of?*

John found the nearest coffee shop, unpacked his MacBook, and connected to the Internet. He enjoyed the sounds of a bustling coffee shop, the clinks of the espresso machines, the various names of people called out by the baristas, and the back and forth of people entering and exiting to get their fix throughout the day. He found a cozy table in the corner, and logged into the Secretary of State's website. It was time to birth this company.

He clicked on the button that read: "Incorporate your business," and followed the prompts until he reached the page requiring the name of his company. He proudly typed in: *T-E-L-O-S.* He then paid the $150.00 incorporation fee, and with just a few more clicks, saw a message pop up in his email box with the following words in all bold: "Congratulations on your incorporation."

As John saw the words flash on the screen, he felt an overwhelming amount of emotion. It felt as if this was the first day of the rest of his life. Tears welled up in his eyes, and John smiled, chuckled, and decided to start searching the web for different companies. He was left feeling extremely engaged in the question posed by Tom. He hadn't thought about the fabric of his being, but he knew that, deep inside, he was a wild animal ready to be unleashed on the business world.

John knew his next step would be to develop an engaging and informative website, explaining his business and offerings. He thought this to be somewhat backwards, as he didn't even have a product to tout. However, he knew that the image of your company often came before the actual company, so he planned to create the sizzle early on. John wasn't quite sure where to start, but Sri provided him with his favorite website developer a few days before ago. John emailed back and forth with the lead account manager, and he asked for some examples of websites John particularly liked. Rick, the account manager, let John know the best way to create your own vision is to model it after the vision of others. He jokingly said, "We all steal from one another, so you might as well start early."

In response to this query, John felt he was as ready as he would ever be to start sculpting Telos. He went to Google.com and typed in the keyword search: "purposeful business." He saw over 1 million results. Somehow, that was both very comforting and extremely overwhelming. But, more than anything, it was nice to know those keywords rang true for so many current and operating organizations. He started clicking on the top few results, surfing their sites, and exploring the verbiage on their homepages. He assumed that he would find the most accurate and clear presentation of their mission and the DNA of their existence.

But, after about an hour of review, he noticed that very few companies clearly stated their purpose and their fundamental pillars. It was as if they were unclear of their existence, using powerful words that really had no meaningful depth. John felt like he wasn't getting much from scouring the Internet, so he decided to look through Sri's connection list on LinkedIn. It was then that he came across Anthony Kittel, the CEO of REDARC. He reviewed Anthony's resume and enjoyed a brief assessment of his bio. It read:

REDARC is a family-owned, technology-based company that designs, manufactures and provides patented, reliable and fully integrated portable vehicular power solutions and customer-centric after sales service to customers in Australia, New Zealand, France, and North America. REDARC's products are technologically-advanced and capable of being fitted to anything with a battery that moves.

Bob Mackie founded REDARC in 1979. Bob was an electronics engineer and started the business in his back room. When Bob passed away in 1995, his wife, Margaret, ran the business under management until 1997. In 1997, Anthony and Michele Kittel purchased REDARC — they invested in a company that had lost its way. Anthony took a salary cut, risked his family home, and knew little about electronics, but he identified the potential in the power-conversion manufacturer. He empowered his staff with a "No Questions Asked" customer warranty and turned the company around during a tough period.

John thought this to be music to his ears. It aligned with every single piece of advice he'd received over the past two weeks. This company and its CEO were passionate, dedicated, and completely clear on its goals. So much so that you felt it as you read it. REDARC was a company to be modeled after, and John couldn't wait to see if he could get Anthony on the phone, even if he had to foot the bill for a phone call to Australia.

"You cannot dream yourself into a character; you must hammer and forge yourself one."
— Henry David Thoreau

John reached out to Sri and explained his current situation. He eventually asked if Sri would make an intro to Anthony.

Sri said, "I will be more than happy to make an introduction to Anthony — he will be perfect for what you are looking for." Shortly thereafter, Sri sent an email and introduced John.

Anthony's open-door policy apparently reached to the consumers, as he made it clear in his mission statement he would be more than willing to accept any email or phone call from the general public. He truly wanted to improve, and the best way to do that was through direct feedback.

It took Anthony only thirty minutes to respond to Sri's email. And the response: "Would love to talk. You available now?"

John was excited that Anthony was so quick to connect, but he had a feeling Anthony was always this way. It was just part of his makeup. John called REDARC, and was quickly patched through to Anthony. He started by thanking Anthony for his time, explained how he found REDARC, and brought Anthony up to speed. John felt he was a pro on the elevator speech, able to bring people into his world in just a couple minutes. He focused on it over the past few weeks, and he recognized that, when given the chance, he would only have a few minutes, so he had to make them count.

Almost immediately after John finished, Anthony said, "Well that is quite a journey — sounds similar to mine. I was somewhat lost, but saw an opportunity and took it. That was when I purchased REDARC. I really didn't know anything about technology, and certainly was clueless on how to run a big business, which REDARC is now. But I focused on the core principles I would apply to any company, whether it was a mom and pop restaurant or Fortunate 500 company. As you can see, it worked out pretty well. But I work every day to continually define and redefine why I do what I do. If you forget to survey the fabric of your makeup, you'll eventually forget why you do what you do."

"I appreciate you sharing that with me," John responded. "Based just on what I read on your site, it seems like you are remarkably focused on your core values. Would you mind sharing with me some of the steps you take on a daily basis to ensure you continuously stay on course?"

"That's a tough question to answer. But let me tell you one of my favorite stories, and one I often reference to my employees.

"Johnson and Johnson, the creators of Tylenol, offer a great example of the importance of having values that actually mean something. In 1982, it was found that Tylenol was inadvertently laced with cyanide. This tragic event resulted in six deaths in Chicago. When it was deemed that Tylenol was the culprit, without hesitation, Johnson and Johnson recalled every single bottle of Tylenol on the market. They paid over $100 million to destroy over 31 million capsules. Now, they had the ability to determine the impacted areas, but rather than picking and choosing, they sent a very clear message to the consumer: we value safety over profit.

"Larry Foster, Corporate Vice President of Public Relations at Johnson & Johnson said, in reflecting on the crises, said: 'What began as Johnsons & Johnson's darkest hour turned out to be its brightest in terms of corporate reputation.'

"When probed further, did he respond to a plan? His response was visionary.

"'No, not really. We responded from our values,' he said."

"Character is like a tree and reputation is like its shadow.
The shadow is what we think of it; the tree is the real thing."
— Abraham Lincoln

John exhaled. "That is amazing. I had no clue. Even in a time of great crisis, it is wonderful to know they remained true to their core values."

"Right. I work hard to do the same. From 12 years of age, I would work with my grandfather at his garage in Hawker, Flinders Ranges, South Australia during every school holiday. This work gave me a great sense of responsibility, and really sparked my interest in owning and running my own business. I believe that passion is the burning desire and motivation to achieve your goals. This desire and motivation comes from within and is self-generating, it is like a fire burning within oneself that drives for success.

"I am passionate about innovation and product development. Nothing gives me more satisfaction than developing a product that customers love and ask for by name. I am also passionate about establishing a culture in the business that allows people to enjoy coming to work every day. I want our staff to jump out of bed with a spring in their step and look forward to coming to work and giving their best every day. If we can provide a learning environment that allows people to develop and maximize their potential through continuous and lifelong learning, then we will have a great business. We recognize that good 'corporate citizenship' extends beyond simply abiding by the law. We seek to behave ethically and to improve quality of life for our workforce, families and the broader community whilst pursuing strong economic performance. There are a few core principles I hold dear to my heart, and I intend to demonstrate those on a daily basis. Some of my favorites, which I constantly try to project to my team of employees, are:

- ✓ **Culture.** I want to ensure that our people thrive on a culture of innovation, family values, and excellence. I believe that 'culture eats strategy for breakfast' and a strong culture is the foundation to any great business. At REDARC, our staff sees themselves as valued employees who make an important contribution to the business's ongoing success.

✓ **Innovation**. We focus on the ongoing personal development of all staff to nurture our innovative company culture. Being a technology-focused business, our entire business model is based upon innovation.

✓ **Customer Satisfaction.** It is important to deliver exceptional after-sales service to be the best in the market. I strongly believe that the 'customer is king' and every activity of doing business should add value, not cost, for the customer. We want to delight the customer and treat them as we personally would like to be treated.

✓ **Teamwork.** We guarantee quality products delivered on time through excellence in cross-functional integration. It is important to work as a team and not in silos. Eliminating politics within the business is crucial so that people are not trying to 'second guess' what or how they should be responding.

✓ **Integrity**. REDARC forges strong relationships with stakeholders, and always acts with the utmost integrity. Trust in business is critical, and if you break the seal of trust, then it is almost impossible to recover this. The key to integrity is 'always doing what you say you will do.' Your word is your bond!

✓ **Quality.** You have to do things right the first time. Quality is key to delivering the customer value for money. If it is worth doing, then it is worth doing it right the first time and giving 100% to the task.

✓ **Environmentally Aware**. We go beyond compliance and are socially responsible in business. We want to ensure that we pass on the earth to the next generation and the generations to come in a better way than we found it."

"Values are like fingerprints, nobody's are the same, but you leave them all over everything you do."
— Elvis Presley

"I know that I just rattled those off, but it is so easy for me to share with you our fundamental beliefs. I wake up each and every day and work to build structure that supports each of these. There are probably more, but I know that these are my bread and butter. Without them, we would simply fold. I think each and every business has to know its DNA, that which encompasses their inner-existence. Without this knowledge, you are just flying blind, and you'll eventually crash."

John felt overwhelmed with excitement. He knew Anthony was the type of guy he could model himself after.

He said, "Anthony, thank you so much. It is not only inspiring to know that there are companies like yours operating at a high level, but I find it extremely impressive that you are so abundantly clear on your core values. I am willing to bet it took you a lot of time to figure these out, and you probably have changed them time and time again — "

Anthony interrupted him, "John, I have to run and really appreciate you reaching out. But I have to tell you one thing…and you have to remember this no matter what you do. It did not take me any time at all to focus these values. I have not changed them even once. I was born with these, I have lived my life by these, and I started my business to fit these specific concepts. I believed I'd succeed in any business I started for the sole reason that these fundamental pillars would be its birthright. Start with your fabric, and build your business to fit it...not the other way around."

John felt overcome with excitement. He was ready to dive into his own fundamental core concepts. These were important, as they would act as the foundation for the large house that was about to be built. From his conversation with Anthony, he identified three areas of interest:

1. Experiences
2. Beliefs
3. Behavior

He figured it was these three points that defined who he was at his core. So, he started to think about his life experiences, his strongest beliefs, and his regular behavior or habits. John recognized most of these go back to his childhood, and many were likely formed early on. In reality, John assumed if he could evaluate the link between his earliest experiences and his most recent strides, he likely would see a pattern. So, he took out his journal, and began to write down some extremely important questions he felt he should consider:

Some of the earliest experiences in my life that have impacted me the most today are...

1. _____

_____

2. _____

_____

3. _____

_____

4. _____

_____

5. _____
_____

My strongest beliefs consist of...

1. _____
_____

2. _____
_____

3. _____
_____

4. _____
_____

5. _____
_____

The behaviors that I regularly participate in which I am most proud of are...

1. _____
_____

2. _____
_____

3. _____
_____

4. _____
_____

5. _____
_____

My Core Values are....

1. _____
_____

2. _____
_____

3. _____
_____

4. _____
_____

5. _____
_____

"Begin each day with the blue print of my deepest values firmly in mind, then when challenges come, make decisions based on those values"
— **Stephen Covey**

John reviewed the answers to his questions, and realized he had a pretty good life, but it was not all rainbows and butterflies. More than anything, John thought these experiences helped or hurt in shaping his belief system, which then led to his decisions and ultimate actions. As John began to jot down the answers to these questions, he thought he was getting just a little bit closer in determining what he was truly made of.

CHAPTER 5:

LESSON #5: SELF AWARENESS & SELF DISCIPLINE:

Identify your Strengths, Weaknesses and Blind Spots

"Strength does not come from winning. Your struggles develop your strengths. When you go through hardships and decide not to surrender, that is strength."
— **Arnold Schwarzenegger**

John felt alive. He had come so far. It felt like a lifetime had passed since he decided to rethink his existence, and search for great purpose. It wasn't easy to this point, but John felt now, more than ever, he made the right decision. There was no turning back now. He accomplished a great deal over the past few weeks. He had found passion in his life, and focused on creating a journey that held purpose higher than profits. John intimately connected with the law of attraction, and realized the remarkable role it could play within his own life. Finally, he evaluated his core values, and considered those characteristics and skills that encompassed the fabric of his existence. It was crazy to think of all that he experienced, as well as the amazing group of people who helped him along the way.

But John also recognized he had a long road ahead. So many steps behind, yet so many more ahead. However, John felt comforted by the fact that this all felt right. He knew his destination got closer and closer by the day, and he was firmly entrenched in his undeniable desire to get there, one way or another. John knew he acquired an enormous amount of information, but still wondered what he hadn't yet learned. It was in his nature to always wonder, and question what he didn't quite understand. He felt like he maintained a strong discipline towards his goals, but to achieve his goals as an entrepreneur requires more than a discipline of focusing on his goal. It was likely a combination of never being here before, and not focusing nearly enough on his perceived blind spots. His mind was wandering in different directions on how and where to get started. What if he went wrong?

To that end, John decided to do something about it. He reached out to Sri and explained his current situation.

Sri said, "Don't worry — everyone goes through this phase; it's an entrepreneur's dilemma. John, let me reach out to Dev Chanchani, a very good friend of mine, and also a classmate from HBS. I will explain to him what you are going through before you reach out to him. I've known Dev for a few years, and I can't think of anyone else better than Dev to address this problem of yours. Give me a day or two and expect an email from me."

Dev is the CEO of INetU, Inc., which was founded on a set of core principles that have guided the business's success and strong growth for nearly 16 years. Dev's business and economics background, combined with years of business experience, successfully promote INetU's industry-respected products and high customer satisfaction levels. Dev has been recognized for his success as a business leader through the Ernst and Young Entrepreneur of the Year program, in which he was a semi-finalist. He holds a Bachelor's degree in Business and Economics from Lehigh University and most recently studied at the Harvard Business School in the OPM Program.

John enjoyed Dev's profile, reading it through twice.

John knew he was running a marathon. And with each leg came another mentor and expert to provide him with the energy required to get him just a little bit closer to the finish line. John started checking his email every couple of hours, desperately looking for Sri's email. Two days later, it finally it arrived in his in-box with the contact details for Dev. John sent an email to Dev requesting a meeting or phone call.

He loved that Dev built a company focused on the consumer. As obvious as it may seem, far too many companies in today's business arena forget just how important the consumer is to their success. Without a consumer of some sort, businesses cannot thrive, or even survive for that matter. They'll wither away and die. Regardless, it felt refreshing that Dev understood who buttered his bread, and highlighted the importance of the consumer to his team. John thought Dev would be a perfect mentor, and decided to contact him immediately.

It took Dev a few days to get back in touch with John. John took those days to decompress. He enjoyed a few long jogs through the parks, visited with friends over coffee, and caught up on a little bit of shopping. John hadn't realized how little time he spent on other areas of his life, as he was singularly focused on his new-founded purpose. But it felt refreshing to cross these items off of his list. After he had replaced the hinge, John checked his email. He saw a response from Dev. He perked up, felt that same elevated heartbeat he did each time a new mentor responded, and opened up the email from Dev.

> *Dear John,*
>
> *Thanks for the nice email. Sri explained to me about your current situation. I am glad to meet you, and I would be more than happy to chat with you about your journey. I have a 60-minute window tomorrow at noon. Are you free for a call? If so, please confirm, and I will have my assistant set it up. Looking forward to our time together. I am at your disposal.*
>
> *— Dev*

John smiled and felt excited about this new opportunity. Over the past few days, and in between his runs and coffee breaks, he had spent a little time reading more about Dev. He learned Dev recently agreed to sell his company to a competitor for $162.5 million dollars. He hoped to discuss that process and experience with Dev. He quickly responded to Dev's email, confirming the time and providing his number to connect.

"Build up your weaknesses until they become your strong points."
— Knute Rockne

John answered his phone on the second ring, eagerly anticipating his call with Dev. He greeted Dev's secretary, who asked him to hold for Dev. Shortly thereafter, a warm and friendly voice came on the line.

"Hey, John," Dev said.

John responded, "Dev, thanks so much for connecting with me. I am so lucky to speak with an expert like you."

"No problem, John — my pleasure. How can I help you through your journey?"

"I guess...well, let me start by asking you...how did you build a successful business?"

"That's a good question. It isn't an easy one to answer, but I will try to share with you some of the most fundamental concepts I focused on. I recently did an interview and the conversation was on customer service. It really got me thinking about how companies use their resources and efforts on their customers. I was asked a bunch of questions, but I think the best content I shared revolved around understanding your strengths and weaknesses, which leads you to a better ability to identify your blind spots. I am a huge fan of building a customer-centric business. That means that everything you do, everything you say, and every decision you make is based off of and geared towards the customer.

"Many companies today claim to offer excellent customer service. When it comes down to it, however, some of those same companies are afraid to give anything up in order to make themselves truly customer-centric. All businesses are caught between three significant motivators that are often at odds with one another:

1. Customers
2. Products
3. Operations

"While all of these elements are important, resolving the tension between them by choosing which is most important to you and your business is the key to success. You will need to make some sacrifices on one front in order to improve on another. In other words, if your goal is to be truly customer-centric, you may need to make some sacrifices when it comes to your product or your operations. As frightening as it may sound to put the customer above your own products or operations, I have experienced first-hand the power of a genuinely customer-centric business model since founding INetU over a decade and a half ago. It comes down to trust and respect. If you focus on creating a company that revolves around the customer experience — one where you think of your customers as an extension of your business, and vice versa — it builds long-lasting relationships, and fosters trust that converts customers into advocates for your business.

"The problem here is that most companies do not assess how they interact and relate to their customers. They don't consider their strengths, their weaknesses, and their blind spots. So, I have worked to craft a few very important questions leaders can ask to determine the emphasis they place on the customer. They are so basic, but have remarkably lasting impact. Let me share those questions with you:

"I think self-awareness is probably the most important thing towards being a champion."
— Billie Jean King

1. Is the customer happy with your service?

"This is an example of self-awareness. This may seem like an obvious question, but you'd be surprised at how many companies don't ask their staff or the customers themselves if the customer is happy, on a regular basis. Rather than looking at financial data, sales and profits, your first question should be about customer satisfaction. At INetU, for example, our senior management meets and reports on what's happening with various customers on a daily basis. If there's anything unusual happening with their infrastructure that day, the first thing I ask is whether the customer is still happy. If they are, we're doing our jobs well. If they're not, we may need to take a step back and make a change to our operations or product.

"In addition to the day-to-day interactions that our staff has with customers, we also make a point to get certified verification of our standing on an annual basis with a Net Promoter Score (NPS). Our NPS consistently lands us among the ranks of Apple, Nordstrom and Zappos, which is great 3rd-party validation that we're delivering an excellent experience to our customers.

2. Is customer-centricity built into your company DNA?

"This is an example of self-discipline. Customer-centric isn't just something you can call yourself; it should be reflected in every aspect of your business — from the company mission to the values of your employees. You have to dedicate yourself to it each and every day. At INetU, we have a fairly long hiring process. I believe it shows candidates that we are committed to them. You can't force someone to be customer-centric, but those that believe in being outwardly focused will understand and respect the process, and will be that much more likely to think long-term once they come onboard. We continue to invest in our employees once they are part of our team, investing in their training and exposing them to the biggest and best ideas and people via conferences and events.

"When it comes to company meetings and reporting, we don't rely on the standard numbers and metrics, such as the number of tickets processed or the time spent on each ticket, in order to measure success. We don't want our customer service team avoiding the tough tickets that will be time-consuming just to keep their numbers up. We encourage a new mindset with our employees — we want our team to own the customer's happiness and work to solve their problems, even if their problems are no fault of ours. We rate our team's performance by allowing customers to rate how well each ticket was handled and provide feedback. If all our team is thinking about is the numbers, then we're missing out on the intangible part of the puzzle that being customer-centric is all about.

3. Are you asking your customers the right questions?

"This is an example of assessing your blind spots. When a customer comes to you in need of your goods or services, you might ask them, 'What do you need?' The right question is actually, 'What problems are you trying to solve?' Customers will often know their pain points, but your business should have the answers when it comes to developing an effective solution for them.

"In that same vein, coming to customers with your latest product and asking, 'Do you need this?' is not the right way for sales teams to operate in a customer-centric business. A better question is, 'What would make your lives easier/better?' At INetU, we have a 'chief hosting officer' designated to each customer. By asking what we can do to make the customer's life easier rather than trying to sell them on our products, we're able to introduce them to capabilities and products that they may not have known we had, while still adding value to their business.

"You've heard the saying, 'The customer is always right.' I have a saying: 'The customer is always right, but not everyone is the right customer.' Some customers may not need you to be as hands-on or attentive. Some may need to let you go for budget reasons. Some may hire a new contact that wants to change things up.

"There are many acceptable reasons to part ways with a customer, but customer-centric organizations should never, ever lose a customer for a service reason. If you do, it's time to reexamine your business and make some changes."

John breathed deeply and responded, "These are extremely thoughtful questions. I love how you have broken them down to analyze your strengths, weaknesses, and blind spots. I really think they help you become more self-aware and disciplined. It is certainly not easy. But I recognize now, more than ever, that you have to understand where you excel, where you fall short, and what you don't know, you don't know."

"That's right," Dev said. "I wish I could take full credit for these. The questions are all mine, and we work meticulously to instill them into our organization, but they are applicable to any aspect of your business or even your life. You should always ask questions that assess three things:

1. What do you do great?
2. What can you improve?
3. What are you missing?

> *"Self-discipline is an act of cultivation. It requires you to connect today's actions to tomorrow's results. There's a season for sowing, a season for reaping. Self-discipline helps you know which is which."*
> **— Gary Ryan Blair**

"These answers will offer you enormous perspective. I read a great blog right before this interview. An author named Sudhir Krishnan[1] wrote it. He was asked what it takes to be the best. His response has offered me great insight. I am going to read it to you.

"It takes three qualities to be 'the best':

1. *A Sense of Purpose*
2. *Self-Awareness*
3. *Discipline*

1. A Sense of purpose:

"Say you just bought your first car. You have no plans to get anywhere at the moment, and so you drive around your area, simply choosing locations you like, and avoiding the locations you do not like. Surely you are spending your time, money, and resources, but since you don't have a plan of direction, you do not really get anywhere. Not having a sense of purpose in life is the same as this. Life becomes meaningful only when a person is driven by a high goal that is guiding you. A sense of purpose provides the undying passion and steadfast commitment to do what you need to do. It gives you worthy goals to strive for. Say you decide to drive your car from New York to Los Angeles. Now this has become your purpose, a goal that guides your actions.

---

1   https://www.facebook.com/pg/SudhirKrishnanFan/notes/

2. Self-Awareness:

"We prepare for our drive to Los Angeles. At each point of the trip we need to generally head west and towards Los Angeles. If we turn north, south, or east for too long, we are unlikely to get to the final destination, despite the purpose/goal we have set for ourselves. When in the car, the GPS or a map provides a sense of direction. The equivalent of the GPS in our life is self-awareness. Many times, due to lack of self-awareness, we head east when we should be really heading west, according to our goals. All action done when lacking skill, lacking knowledge or under the influence of negative emotions can be classified as a lack of self-awareness. Due to a lack of self-awareness, we self-sabotage the materialization of our own goals. Self-awareness also provides input to selecting your life's purpose, as a person with self-awareness selects goals that are in alignment with who he really is.

3. Discipline:

"Say we have both a sense of purpose and self-awareness for our trip to Los Angeles. We know where we want to go, and whether we are currently headed in the right direction or not. Even with the above two being present, there can be many distractions along the path. While on your trip, you may get the idea to go and visit various other places, some of which may be along the path, and some that may be detours, and some that may be completely opposite to your goal/purpose of reaching Los Angeles. If you give in to too many temptations and have many detours, then you are unlikely to reach the goal you have set for yourself. Discipline is the act of cultivating habits that are in alignment with your higher goal/purpose, so that even when there is temptation to go off-track, you stay steadfast and keep progressing on the goal you have set for yourself."

"John, this is a pretty basic example. We have all gone on a road trip. But the concepts he outlines are powerful stuff. I wake up each and every day and attempt to figure out how I can do better, how I can maintain quality, and search for the answers I did not even know I needed. It is a lifelong journey. I want to know how I can get to my destination without wasting gas, without getting lost, and without losing focus of the road ahead."

John thoroughly enjoyed his conversation with Dev. The guidance and feedback were remarkable. They offered John perspectives he had never quite considered; three simple questions that could unlock so many doors. He took out his journal and began to jot down notes from his call with Dev. He wrote down the following:

Every business has to focus on three things:

1. *Identify Your Strengths: What do you do great?*
2. *Recognize Your Weaknesses: What can you improve?*
3. *Evaluate Your Blind Spots: What are you missing?*

> *"Mature striving is linked to long-range goals. Thus, the process of becoming is largely a matter of organizing transitory impulses into a pattern of striving and interest in which the element of self-awareness plays a large part. "*
> **Gordon W. Allport**

John had yet to open the doors to his business, but he quickly recognized the important points Dev offered. He would have to spend considerable time addressing each of these issues in his newly formed business. After his conversation with Dev, one other point stood out in his mind: focus on the customer. John thought it ironic that, in this day and age, businesses still forgot that it is your customers that keep you in business, or can put you out of it. He decided he would build a company that was customer-centric, and strived to connect and learn from the customer. Again, John felt excited and was interested in sharing this great conversation with Sri. He decided it had been a long day, and likely too late to contact Sri. He'd reach out to him in the morning.

CHAPTER 6:

LESSON #6: THE BALANCE OF OPPORTUNITY-COST:

Is the Risk Worth the Reward?

"A ship is always safe at shore—but that is not what it is built for."
— **Albert Einstein**

L ooking back, it was an amazing six-month journey since John first incorporated his business. John had been busy working with his core team of three people for the last 150 days to develop the educational software. In addition, he relied upon one domain expert and two programmers. He was very satisfied with their progress, and they were able to successfully develop the prototype and present it to few potential educational institutions. Most of the institutions were interested in adopting TELOS software and ready to sign a Memorandum of Understanding (MOU) as beta customers to test the product in order to get started.

John always knew there was a need and substantial pain in the market, but was really excited to see such a great response. However, the challenge for him was that he did not have enough resources to implement all the sites or customers. He also needed his core team to work for another three — six months onsite to complete the launch.

The challenge for John was that he definitely needed two or three beta customers to get their inputs and complete the product, but had almost ten other customers who wanted to get involved. He hated the idea of telling them no, fearing he would lose them forever. He wondered if he should reach out to private equity investors or angel investors to help grow his team and meet the demand? He couldn't figure out if the risk was worth the reward.

John called Sri the next day. He enjoyed recapping his journey to date, and they discussed the remarkable people John had met and the transparent and exciting conversations he had with them.

John said, "I am most impressed with how willing these people are to share. They share their stories, their insight, and their amazing journeys with me. It feels so inspiring that people are just willing to help others succeed. I assumed I would be lucky enough to receive some meaningful feedback from these mentors, but this is more than I could ever expect."

"Think nothing of it," Sri responded. "As humans, we are destined to collaborate, to help one another, to join together and allow our journeys to become our collective destinations. I believe there are actually more people that want to help than those that are unwilling to do so. The work is cyclical, John. It is literally one big circle. We are all together, and we are all part of the natural growth and development, whether we want to be or not. So why not band together and allow progress to become a common goal?"

"That makes sense. I truly recognize that. Thanks again for all of your continued guidance."

John explained to Sri about his current opportunity and the risk coming with it.

Sri simply smiled and said, "John we all learn from our own mistakes. If you have a good network or continuous learning attitude, you can learn faster from others' experiences. But at this juncture, it's too risky for you to make any mistakes.

"In my experience, successful people have a very good intuition in identifying the right opportunities based on their experiences and competencies. This occurs at both an individual and organizational level. In fact, most people have great ideas or have come across many opportunities in life. But very few people will make it big. You have to leave your comfort zone to successfully accomplish your goals by taking calculated risks.

"The biggest difference between success and failure is that successful people are determined to succeed, no matter what they do. When they come across an opportunity, they take action in a timely manner while considering potential risks. Others keep chasing perfection before they act due to fear of failure. They eventually lose focus and move on to a new idea. Then it is too late to act on it. Once successful people decide to pursue their desired goal, they consciously think about it around the clock and build a strong network that is aligned with their vision. They reach out to it when needed. But not before they assess the risk versus the reward.

"For instance, we viewed the recession as a great business opportunity. So, we increased our company's sales and delivery force while several competitors were decreasing theirs. As a result of this intuitive decision, ERP Analysts aggressively marketed 'Fixed Bid,

Not to Exceed' and 'Free Assessment' strategies with its increased sales force to attract new customers during a time of great uncertainty in the market. This aggressive strategy not only helped the company gain market share, but it also earned a loyal lifetime number of customers who view the company as a true partner that stood by them during adversity."

"I love it," John responded. "Thanks for all the insight Sri."

"Let me introduce you to another classmate of mine: Enrique Gonzalez from HBS, who has a lot to offer you from his own experience.

Enrique is the CEO and driving force behind IPVG, and he oversaw a vast IT empire composed of data centers, call centers, online games, IT security, and e-payment products. What interests me the most about him is that, in 2012, he decided to forego his experience and empire he built in IT, and invested over a quarter of a billion dollars in a mining investment and operation in the United States. He went all-in. He asked for his board of directors to amend the bylaws of his company to allow for such a drastic change in business practice. On its face, it almost seemed crazy. When you asked about opportunity vs. risk, immediately Enrique came to my mind. I've got to figure out a way to get Enrique on the phone. I will update you tomorrow."

"Once again, thanks for being an unbelievable mentor to me."

Sri said, "We are in this together — no one can do it alone. Chat with you soon."

"Life is either a daring adventure or nothing at all."
— Helen Keller

Excited to chat with Enrique, John reached out. "Enrique, thanks so much for agreeing to take a call from me. I enjoyed our emails this week. I keep meeting amazing people whose stories inspire my own journey. The most fascinating part is your very extreme and sudden change in the course of your business. You were so successful doing one thing, and you gave it up for another. What led you down that path?"

Enrique responded, "John, ever hear of cost vs. reward?"

John said, "Of course — I discussed this with Sri yesterday."

"Good. Then this should make sense. Fundamentally, the cost was worth the reward. From the beginning, I focused on early stage investments and propositions. We are always geared for growth. We spend 90% of our time looking forward and 10% looking backward and learning from past mistakes. We then quickly apply this into how we operate. We build teams that can move fast and achieve results at a high rate. Success of a start-up depends on its ability to adapt and move fast. Like a small animal, our advantage is not size but speed. Therefore, we are always focused on capturing as much growth as we can.

"Funnily enough, one of my potentially biggest failures was in the mining industry. We entered with a contrarian view and got caught in a much longer downward cycle on both a global and local level. We couldn't have seen it coming. We also made 'fatal' mistakes in our first year by having the wrong management team and the incorrect business plan. We ran out of capital in our second year. Most people would have given up. We persevered and are currently thriving. We adjusted our business model and plan from being an operator to a concession owner. We secured two foreign partners who would operate in different parts of the mine. We are currently scheduled to commence production in the near future. Living in a daily crisis forces you to focus on survival. You have to prioritize, persevere and remain extremely patient. We may not meet our intended goal within our original timelines, but sometimes we have to be able to shift from the short game to long game without losing your cool and morale. Needless to say, it has not been easy."

> *"Failure is simply the opportunity to begin again, this time more intelligently."*
> **— Henry Ford**

"Before we do anything, we take the time assess the opportunity. It is suicide not to. There are two steps every businessman should take before making a decision:

1. Carefully review the opportunity
2. Create a strong business plan

"While there is no such thing as a bulletproof business plan, a good plan is the closest realization to your vision before the execution begins. It ensures that every part of the company is paddling the canoe in the same direction. Harnessing the power of your organization to push towards the same goal can spell the difference between success and failure. It is where good separates from great. At the end of the day, you cannot do it all. You have to make a choice. Scarcity at its finest. There is this great economist, Daniel Kurt[2], and he said:

> 'The idea of scarcity lies at the heart of economics. It's the concept that, in virtually every decision we make, we face constraints. In short, humans don't have the money, skills, time — you name it — to get everything we possibly desire. Ergo, we have to make choices. Economists are keen to remind

---

2   web.utah.edu/basford/.../WhatIsOpportunityCostAndWhyDoesItMatter.docx

us that decisions don't take place in a vacuum. Life isn't only about the choices we make, but the ones we could make. This is where something called opportunity cost *comes into play. It's the term social scientists use to describe the value of the next best alternative to the option we're considering.*

We actually evaluate opportunity costs on a daily basis. Perhaps when you woke up today, you decided on a big bowl of cereal for breakfast, foregoing the opportunity to enjoy eggs and toast. A little later, you opt to take the train to work, sacrificing the benefits of driving your own car. It's still early morning, and you've already decided on a series of small tradeoffs.

Calculating opportunity costs may seem like a no-brainer when the only objective is to increase the bottom line. No successful company is going to reinvest its earnings without considering the financial effects of different options. Because of the scarcity of resources, saying yes *to one option necessarily means saying* no *to the alternatives. To make the best decision, one has to consider the value of those other options, too.*

Every year I seem to have the same resolution: say no *more often.'*

"When you start a business, your resources are the most valuable tools you have in your possession. Every dollar spent here is a dollar less to spend there. But once you have a point of security, you can be much pickier. In short, you evaluate cost vs. reward in a different light. It is critical to have a basic understanding of yourself as a business owner and also your business as a whole so that you can prioritize your resources. Once established, you have to figure out where your primary focus should be. I once heard, 'Profitability is determined by finding the balance between ease of producing products or administrating services, all costs associated with them, and the revenue from sales and other investments.'

"It's funny: if a factory can produce more chairs than tables during an hour, then priority should be given to making chairs over tables, right? Well, we decided that IT was no longer our focus, even though that is probably the path of least resistance. Opportunity cost can be complex, but good business owners ask themselves, 'What is the opportunity cost of a decision?' Now, the answer may seem nonsensical at first, but if you remain focused and dedicated to exactly *why* you made that decision, you'll find a better path to success. I have always defined 'passion' as having an almost crazy zeal and commitment to achieving a vision. I am most passionate about building a business that can scale and last, that can serve a need and solve a problem, and of course be rewarded with profits. So, I felt the mining industry is my best chance to scale. I may be right, I could be wrong…but the cost is worth the reward to me."

John said, "That makes sense. But, are you scared you are wrong? Are you concerned your team will decide this path is just too crazy a journey for them?"

"Good questions. Of course there is some doubt. But I found purpose gives meaning to both the journey and the destination. It is very important to me that anyone I hire into the company (especially at the management level) completely and absolutely understands our purpose. If they don't, we aren't for them and they are not for us. We instill this through clear and constant communication, through hands on mentorship and training, and practicing what we preach. So to that end, we have already completed the opportunity cost analysis. That ship has sailed. We decided this sudden turn in our business model is the right move for us. So, now we move to the execution part of the game plan. And if you aren't part of the vision, you just aren't the right fit for us.

"As entrepreneurs, we see what others do not, and in the process of our work and success, we re-shape the world we live in. Clarity of vision is extremely important when creating something out of nothing. Having a clear vision anchors you towards your goal and allows you to measure very clearly where you are versus where you want to be. I do not start or invest in a vision unless it is very clear. The ability to visualize has allowed me to enter over seven different sectors successfully. Mining will be my eighth. And in each journey, I assessed the risk versus the reward, and made my decision on gut instincts as well as measurables."

"The biggest risk is not taking any risk. In a world that changing really quickly, the only strategy that is guaranteed to fail is not taking risks."
— **Mark Zuckerberg**

"I have evolved in many ways. I used to build companies to "flip" them for a quick profit. However, I am now currently building companies that can "last." I used to be ruthlessly focused on results. I am currently more holistic in my current approach, including focusing on human capital development, serving stakeholders and having a purpose beyond making money. I learn and re-learn everyday, considering I specialize in early stage businesses and investments. We learn to succeed on a single unit, and create an organization that can rapidly scale it. Each of these opportunities has its own set of unique risks, so we assess, make an informed decision, and then execute at a high level."

John responded, "That is a remarkable attitude. I can only imagine how difficult it must be to continuously grow, develop, and evolve as a company. I really appreciate the insight you offered me. To boil it down, it seems to me that, when considering the big concept of Cost v. Reward, you have to take a step-by-step approach that includes:

1. Determining the right balance between resources, risk and opportunities.
2. Determining your desire/ability to tolerate risk.
3. Assessing that risk through a well-conceived business plan.
4. Determining what "success" or your reward will look like.
5. Making a decision quickly and with great purpose.
6. Executing your game plan, maintaining focus, and persevering when times get tough.

"Does that sound like a meaningful way to approach the cost versus reward model?"

"Absolutely," Enrique said. "I would tell you that the most important step is to assess the risk. That is crucial to success. But that is unlikely to be the hardest step in your process. That step is maintaining focus and remembering why you made the decision in the first place. With any new endeavor come enormous obstacles and challenges. They may seem like they come from everywhere, and are always flying in your direction. It is extremely easy to doubt your vision, cut the mission short, or just abandon ship entirely. But a little bit of dedication to the purpose can often see you through the tough times. People would tell you I am crazy for trading in an established IT company for an endeavor in mining, but I see great opportunity there, even through the rough terrain."

"The entrepreneur always searches for change, responds to it, and exploits it as an opportunity."
— **Peter Drucker**

John enjoyed his phone call with Enrique. He had thought Enrique would be an interesting mentor, and he certainly delivered. His approach was completely against the grain, and John admired that this man made an informed decision and followed his vision, even if it seemed to be a totally different path. John realized that opportunity existed everywhere, and there should be no boundaries on it. He pulled out his notepad and began to scribble down some notes from his conversation with Enrique. However, one, and only one phrase stood out above the rest.

As he closed his journal, he read that phrase one more time: *"Seek the opportunity; assess the risk; execute the game plan; don't ever look back."*

CHAPTER 7:

LESSON #7: EVOLVING MINDS:

Continuous Learning Develops Unbroken Success

"Education is the kindling of a flame, not the filling of a vessel."

— Socrates

In the last few months, John's team aggressively continued developing the software and decided to work with just two beta customers. John felt it would be best to avoid great risk, and focus resources on doing a great job for just a few customers.

John and his team were able to work with those two customers on a very aggressive schedule and were able to successfully complete the software product to their satisfaction. There were small setbacks along the way, but they handled these with constant tinkering and adjustments. He was working 16-hour days, but he felt he made the right decision by not working with all the interested parties. John thanked Enrique in his mind for the wonderful advice. While his team was testing the software before taking the customers live, John was trying to figure out how to sell, market, and promote the product, while also talking to investors and private equity firms, to help raise more funds to support his business and grow.

John contacted Sri and discussed the newest problem on hand. John indicated that he had to first secure the funds, then he needed to do something about sales, marketing, internal operations and to add resources to continuously work on enhancing the product. He had never worked in these areas, only referencing the education he received at Harvard. Since then, everything had changed. Sales and marketing was more digital as compared to the traditional ways of door-to-door selling.

Sri shared with John, "First of all, I am really happy you were so determined to reach your goal. Your journey has been very successful. You did very well with what you do best, but now you are going to enter the second phase of your entrepreneurial journey, which is dealing with the unknowns, or those obstacles you really don't expect. This phase requires continuous learning and adapting to the fast-changing business dynamics with quick decision-making."

Sri shared an article with John, written and published by David Anderson[3], a business wealth consultant, which read:

> *For many entrepreneurs, continued education efforts are the last thing on their minds. With the hectic responsibilities of running a business, most business owners don't even have time to stop and brew a pot of coffee, let alone invest in a series of continuing education courses or lectures. Still, the benefits of continued education are profound and valuable.*

3   http://www.davidandersonwealth.com/entrepreneurs/10-reasons-why-every-entrepreneur-should-invest-in-continued-education/

Business is a constantly changing and adapting world, and unless an entrepreneur equips himself or herself to ride the tide of change and adapt along with the business community, failure may be inevitable.

However, the needs of an entrepreneur should be considered just as often as the needs of the business. An entrepreneur is the driving force behind a business. When an entrepreneur is edified and educated, the business improves. When an entrepreneur accesses helpful and valuable information, the business benefits. It's unwise to separate the entrepreneur from his or her business and vice versa. Feeding one provides nourishment for the other. In case you're still not convinced, or you're dragging your heels regarding the need to continue your own education, here are five inarguable reasons why every entrepreneur should invest in continued education.

1. The Business World is Changing

First, it's important to acknowledge that the business world is in a constant state of adaptation and dramatic change. Business today is almost unrecognizable when compared with business ten, or even five, years ago. The introduction of social media marketing, the new concept of subdividing a target audience into niches, new forms of business software, and new guidelines for interacting with clients and employees are just a few of the changes that have affected the business community. Without continued education efforts, these changes would be essentially unknown to and unrecognized by an entrepreneur. Entrepreneurs are in the business game for the long haul. Most hope to grow and develop their business over the next several years. Imagine the changes that big businesses like Wal-Mart or Google were forced to deal with over the years. Without continuing education, the brains behind the powerhouses would have been lost.

2. Eliminates the Dinosaur Syndrome

The dinosaur syndrome is something that challenges and threatens even the most successful entrepreneurs. Without continuing education, entrepreneurs are in danger of watching their insights and practices become obsolete right before their eyes. What works today will not work tomorrow. If regular education efforts are not on the docket, an entrepreneur may be treated like a business dinosaur: irrelevant and on his way to becoming extinct.

3. Learn New, Streamlining Techniques

Continuing education isn't just something that can help in principle. With continuing education, entrepreneurs can learn the latest business operation techniques. Many of these techniques are specifically designed to streamline business operations and reduce operational costs so a business can increase profit margins. Investing in continued education may seem like excessive upfront costs, but the cost-saving benefits of learning new, streamlining techniques is undeniable.

4. Learn New Marketing Strategies

The only way to generate more profits within a business is to engage in appropriate and current marketing strategies that have proved to be effective. How, though, will entrepreneurs be apprised of these new and effective marketing strategies without investing in continuing education? Enrolling in *marketing courses, reading articles and blog posts created by industry professionals, and attending seminars are all great ways to learn the latest techniques that can help a business expand its audience and increase its customer population.*

5. Generate Excitement to Replace Exhaustion

Continued education can also serve to re-energize and excite an entrepreneur that has been bogged down by a failing business or increasing obstacles. Information about new business practices, anecdotes from business professionals, and the absorption of new business knowledge can help an entrepreneur rediscover his or her passion for business.

Without continued education, an entrepreneur may become ineffective, uninformed, or out of touch with the effective business practices that will guide his or her business to greater success.

"Education is what remains after one has forgotten what one has learned in school."
— Albert Einstein

John loved this particular article, and read it often. It reminded him of the *why* behind his own journey, and kept him focused on constant development, always reaching out and looking to others for guidance and training.

This time, Sri introduced another HBS classmate of his: Rudy Eyl, President of Breman Capital Group Inc., a Florida-based holding company that specialized in cross-border transactions with Europe and Asia.

As John navigated the company website, he noticed a link entitled "Social Responsibility." He clicked on the link and learned that Breman supported nonprofit organizations to aid in child development and offer educational opportunities to young people with limited resources.

He finished reviewing the website, and then reached out to Rudy. "John — awesome of you to reach out. It is always great to connect with an HBS graduate, and I am extremely impressed with your story and dedication to this new path. One thing that really stood out in your email to my assistant was your continued desire to learn, something I hold dearly in my own heart and career."

"Thanks, Rudy. This has been an enormously helpful educational experience. And I appreciate your willingness to share your thoughts with me."

"That's no problem," Rudy said. "I love talking about the journey. It hasn't always been an easy one, but I firmly believe the lessons along the way lead to enormous growth. For me, life is a continual test to earn eternal life and all of the difficulties in the way are part of the trial. How you respond to adversity is under your control and being a consistent optimist has always allowed me to effectively and consistently find alternatives to solve problems. Everything we do has the purpose of serving others (customers, impoverished kids, and country). Instilling purpose within each other is done by always setting a good example, and you can do this through educating people about the journey."

"Exactly," John said. "Tell me this — what role has education played for you over the years?"

"Good question. I strongly recommend continuous education for every entrepreneur or leader to remain competent and updated constantly in order to make the right business decisions at the appropriate time. At the same time, leaders can advise their key team members on improving their core competencies for mutual benefit. Continuous education improves self-awareness; improving self-awareness goes beyond one's own personal experiences and beliefs. It helps people to make better decisions on various available opportunities and risks."

John responded: "Good point. I never really came to terms with just how important continuous education is to me. That is, until I decided to take another look at where I stood and make a drastic life change; then it all became crystal clear."

"You know John — when it comes to learning, I remain a child. By that, I think children maintain an amazing sense of wonder and discovery. They are wired to be curious, and remain so until that is broken. An entrepreneur's mind should be that of a child, constantly dreaming and searching for great ideas. For example, I made a list to help me with daily education, which consists of:

1. Learning from customers, suppliers, and business partners.
2. Industry-specific news and updates through trade organizations.
3. Participating in industry/personal specific networks, training and trade shows.
4. Business networking peer groups such as Young Presidents' Organization (YPO) or similar groups.
5. Learning from peers, market research and competition.
6. Remaining connected to HBS alumni.
7. Discussing relevant topics and focusing on my team.
8. Surrounding myself with a younger crowd that helps you learn faster.

"Each of these areas of focus keeps me remarkably organized and ensures I continue to progress. I really like to focus on a younger generation, as they are always the most hungry for education. They seem to be on the cutting edge of technology and change, so they seem to identify the next best thing before the rest of us. Whatever the case may be, if you take nothing else away from our conversation, remember that you should always set goals for your educational journey."

John said, "That is great, Rudy. Thank you for sharing that with me. As soon as we get off of our call, I plan to create a game plan for my continued education. I want to evolve and succeed, just like you have. Thank you so much for your time. Would it be ok if I connected with you again in the near future?"

"Of course, John. I enjoyed connecting. Ciao."

"Bye, Rudy. Until the next time."

"Live life as if you were to die tomorrow, and learn as if you were to live forever."
— Mahatma Gandhi

John decided to call Sri and update him on his latest call.

"Hey, John — how are you?"

"Doing great, Sri. I just wanted to update you about a recent call I had with Rudy Eyl. He is a really great guy, and we had a fantastic conversation about the value of continuous learning. We both agreed the enormous value it offers, and how a dedication to education results in unbroken success. Truly great stuff, Sri."

"I totally agree. I am a firm believer in the necessity of maintaining constant devotion and commitment to your educational journey. It never ends. It keeps getting better. A great example of this is the phone company Nokia. Remember them?

"I do," John responded.

"Nokia is a fascinating company. For years upon years, Nokia was an industry leader, paving the way for cellular technology and new devices. However, Microsoft eventually acquired Nokia, mostly because Nokia could not maintain a successful business on its own. Nokia was a respectable company. It didn't do anything wrong in its business. However, the world just changed too fast. Its opponents were too powerful. It just couldn't keep up. So, Microsoft saw an opportunity and jumped on it. In my opinion, Nokia missed out on learning, on changing, and it inevitably lost the opportunity at hand to make it big, and survive the shifting waters. Not only did it miss the opportunity to earn big money, Nokia lost its chance of survival."

"But how do you attribute that to continuous education? Couldn't it just be the environment, the circumstances, the culture, or something else?"

Sri paused and then responded. "Absolutely. However, I know Nokia failed because of a lack of dedication to education. Its own CEO made that abundantly clear. At the press conference to announce the purchase, he closed his speech by saying, 'we didn't do anything wrong, but somehow, we lost.' A statement like that just shows how very blind he was. Losing is indicative of doing something wrong. Sometimes you are not prepared as your competition and sometimes you just get beaten. But if you look at Nokia, it never changed — the company lost, because it decided to maintain the status quo, while the competition was forging ahead and looking for something new."

"Once you stop learning, you start dying."
— Albert Einstein

"It's not wrong if you don't want to learn new things. However, if your thoughts and mindset cannot catch up with time, you will be eliminated — just like Nokia. Nokia taught me a lesson that I follow to this very day: never stop learning. You need education to grow, especially if you are a leader or entrepreneur. For me, I started what I call 'Car University.' I decided, early on, that would use dead time, like when I am stuck in traffic, to learn. I regularly listen to books on audio regarding personal development topics, always trying to learn, even when I am sitting in my car. This is a behavior that I developed over the years. I never focused on any formal education or even read business books until a management consultant showed up at our office and scared us to death. He said that our business was going to collapse if we did not do what he said. It was an eye-opener for us. Though we learned that we needed to do something, we were not immediately ready to implement his recommended changes and could not justify the hefty price tag for his services.

"We understood that we needed to standardize our operational procedures, but it required changing management techniques because it involved a cultural shift. As I came from a technical background myself, I realized that I needed to improve my competencies in business to support further growth and then do the same for other key personnel in the organization to gain a sustained competitive advantage. Then, I decided to go to business school. Business school was my first step toward continuous education. Eventually, I developed an interest in reading leadership and business books related to current opportunities and issues that focused on creating business success. The business knowledge I gained through continuing education helped me to become a better leader. I improved my listening skills by considering various options so as to lead and influence others. I also tried to inspire them to reach their full potential with structured mentoring and executive coaching for me and my team to align them with the culture and goals of the organization.

"But we did not stop there. I also encouraged all my C level staff to sharpen their business skills and improve their management skills. Most of them have completed an MBA program or are going through an MBA program. I also conferred with a few friends and industry experts, seeking their advice, and eventually created a formal advisory board that meets every quarter to discuss various issues on-hand and future opportunities. Regardless of formal or informal education, successful people are always curious to seek solutions to their problems. They continually feed their appetite for knowledge in their focused areas. Their drive is to make intuitive business decisions in identifying and acting on opportunities they come across. Continuing education improved my awareness and created confidence in my ability to make better decisions. All these were helpful in developing and reaching out to my trusted network for advice based on various personal or business situations in life. You are doing the same. A successful person learns from others' experiences while taking advantage of continuing education to formulate frameworks for business strategies, learning from others' mistakes and successes in the past, and training the conscious brain to make intuitive decisions in any given situation."

John said, "That is remarkable. I did not realize how dedicated you were to continuous education. Rudy seemed to have a similar attitude. I was very impressed by his immersive dedication to constantly evolving. What I now know is that successful entrepreneurs are relentless in their pursuit of education and information. There is always so much to learn — you just have to find the right path for you and your life."

*"A man only learns in two ways: one by reading, and the
other by association with smarter people."*
— Will Rogers

John decided he would take out his journal and create a plan for
his educational development. Some of these would include:

1. Attending a sales and marketing workshop in the next 30
   days.
2. Reading and summarizing two self-help or educational books
   related to current issues on-hand.
3. Reading books on company valuations and investments
   before talking to more investment bankers.
4. Creating an advisory board to advise on on-going issues and
   future opportunities.
5. Learning in the car from audiobooks to better utilize time
   while driving.
6. Scheduling and enjoying four mentoring lunches with
   industry experts he respected.
7. Teaching another a new skillset, or helping that person to
   improve an existing one.
8. Publishing at least one article in an academic magazine or
   university paper.
9. Watching at least one documentary on a new topic, industry-
   specific or otherwise.
10. Meditating and/or attending three yoga classes, focusing on
    reflection and thought.

As John completed his list, he was surprised as to how many
different ways he could learn. Some were direct, like reading a book

or chatting with a mentor, while others were more indirect, and called for exploration, discovery, and trying new things. John never fully realized just how many opportunities you have to learn. In the non-traditional sense, learning occurred in so many different ways. In fact, he realized that it is almost impossible not to learn. It takes more effort to avoid the journey than to just let the tides move you along.

"Life is a series of experiences; each one of which makes us bigger, even though sometimes it is hard to realize this. For the world was built to develop character, and we must learn that the setbacks and griefs which we endure help us in our marching onward."
— **Henry Ford**

John closed his journal, satisfied that if he stayed the course, he would position himself for an enormous amount of learning opportunities. Between those conversations he had with both Rudy and Sri, he knew he was well along the way to remain dedicated to the educational journey ahead.

CHAPTER 8:

LESSON #8: BUILDING A WINNING TEAM:

Teamwork Is Success

"No matter how brilliant your mind or strategy, if you're playing a solo game, you'll always loose to a team."
— Reid Hoffman, Co-Founder LinkedIn

ohn clicked through the links, and ended up at Forbes.com. Sri recently sent him a link to an article entitled, *6 Ways Successful Teams are Built to Last[4]*, authored by Glenn Llopis. The screen flickered, and a large grey Forbes.com logo appeared. The site redirected John to a page filled with text, and John dove in headfirst. The article read:

[4] http://www.forbes.com/sites/glennllopis/2012/10/01/6-ways-successful-teams-are-built-to-last/#ce9b932268dd

It takes great leadership to build great teams. Leaders who are not afraid to course-correct, make the difficult decisions and establish standards of performance that are constantly being met — and improving at all times. Whether in the workplace, professional sports, or your local community, team-building requires a keen understanding of people, their strengths and what gets them excited to work with others. Team-building requires the management of egos and their constant demands for attention and recognition — not always warranted. Team-building is both an art and a science and the leader who can consistently build high performance teams is worth their weight in gold.

History has shown us that it takes a special kind of leader with unique competencies and skills to successfully build great companies and teams. In the sports world, the late John Wooden set the standard for great coaches, leading UCLA to ten NCAA national basketball championships in a 12-year period — seven in a row. His success was so iconic, Wooden created his own "Pyramid for Success" to help others excel through his proven wisdom. In the business world, we can look to Jack Welsh, who was the Chairman and CEO of General Electric between 1981 and 2001. According to Wikipedia, the company's value rose 4000% during his tenure. In 2006, Welch's net worth was estimated at $720 million and in 2009, he launched the Jack Welsh Management Institute at Strayer University.

"Teamwork makes the dream work, but a vision becomes a nightmare when the leader has a big dream and a bad team."
— John C. Maxwell

Building companies requires the know-how to build long-lasting teams. This is why most managers never become leaders and why most leaders never reach the highest pinnacle of leadership success. It requires the ability to master the "art of people" and knowing how to maneuver hundreds (if not thousands) of people at the right place and at the right time. It means knowing how each person thinks and how to best utilize their competencies rightly at all times. It's playing a continuous chess match — knowing that every wrong move that is made can cost the company hundreds of thousands, if not millions of dollars (just ask BP and Enron).

As you evaluate the sustainability of the team(s) you lead and its real impact on the organization you serve, here are six ways successful teams are built to last:

1. Be Aware of How You Work

As the leader of the team, you must be extremely aware of your leadership style and techniques. Are they as effective as you think? How well are they accepted by the team you are attempting to lead? Evaluate yourself and be critical about where you can improve, especially in areas that will benefit those whom you are leading. Though you may be in charge, how you work may not be appreciated by those who work for you. You may have good intentions, but make sure you hold yourself accountable to course-correct and modify your approach, if necessary, to assure that you're leading from a position of strength and respectability.

Be your own boss. Be flexible. Know who you are as a leader.

2. Get to Know the Rest of the Team

Much like you need to hold yourself accountable for your actions to assure you maximize performance and results, you must make the time to get to know your team and encourage camaraderie. In my "emotional intelligence blog," I discuss the importance of caring, understanding the needs of your team and embracing differences and helping your colleagues experience their significance. In this case, gathering intelligence means learning what defines the strengths and capabilities of your team — the real assets that each member brings to the table, those they leave behind, and those yet to be developed.

All great leaders know exactly what buttons to push and when to push them. They are experts at activating the talent that surrounds them. They are equally as effective at matching unique areas of subject matter expertise and/or competencies to solve problems and seek new solutions.

Fully knowing your team means that you have invested the time to understand how they are wired to think and what is required to motivate them to excel beyond what is expected from them.

Think of your team as puzzle pieces that can be placed together in a variety of ways.

3. Clearly Define Roles & Responsibilities

When you successfully complete step 2, you can then more effectively and clearly define the roles and responsibilities of those on your team. Now, don't assume this is an easy step; in fact, you'll often find that people's ideal roles lie outside their job descriptions.

Each of your team member's responsibilities must be interconnected and dependent upon one another. This is not unlike team sports, where some players are known as "system players" — meaning that, although they may not be the most talented person on the team, they know how to work best within the "system." This is why you must have a keen eye for talent that can evaluate people not only on their ability to play a particular role — but even more so on whether they fit the workplace culture (the system) and will be a team player.

For example, I once inherited an employee who wasn't very good at his specific job. Instead of firing him, I took the time to get to know him and utilized his natural talents as a strategic facilitator who could keep all of the moving parts within the department in proper alignment and in lock-step communication. This person helped our team operate more efficiently and saved the company money by avoiding the bad decisions they previously made because of miscommunications. He was eventually promoted into a special projects manager role.

A team should operate as a mosaic whose unique strengths and differences convert into a powerful united force.

4. Be Proactive with Feedback

Feedback is the key to assuring any team is staying on track, but more importantly, that it is improving each day. Feedback should be proactive and constant. Many leaders are prone to wait until a problem occurs before they give feedback.

Feedback is simply the art of great communication. It should be something that is part of one's natural dialogue. Feedback can be both formal and informal. In fact, if it becomes too structured and stiff, it becomes difficult for the feedback to be authentic and impactful.

Remember that every team is different, with its own unique nuances and dynamics. Treat them as such. No cookie-cutter approach is allowed. Allow proactive feedback to serve as your team's greatest enabler for continuous improvement.

Take the time to remind someone of how and what they can be doing better. Learn from them. Don't complicate the process of constructive feedback. Feedback is two-way communication.

5. Acknowledge and Reward

With proactive feedback comes acknowledgement and reward. People love recognition, but are most appreciative of respect. Take the time to give your teammates the proper accolades they have earned and deserve. I have seen too many leaders take performance for granted because they don't believe that one should be rewarded for "doing their job."

At a time when people want to feel as if they are making a difference, be a thoughtful leader and reassure your team that you are paying attention to their efforts. Being genuine in your recognition and respect goes a long way towards building loyalty and trust. It organically ignites extra effort!

When people are acknowledged, their work brings them greater satisfaction and becomes more purposeful.

6. Always Celebrate Success

At a time when uncertainty is being dealt with each day, you must take the time to celebrate success. This goes beyond acknowledgment — this is about taking a step back and reflecting on what you have accomplished and what you have learned throughout the journey.

In today's fast-paced, rapidly changing world of work, people are not taking enough time to understand why they were successful and how their success reverberated and positively impacted those around them. I have seen leaders fall into the trap of self-aggrandizement — because of what their teams accomplished — rather than celebrating the success stories that in many cases required tremendous effort, sacrifice and perseverance.

Celebration is a short-lived activity. Don't ignore it. Take the time to live in the moment and remember what allowed you to cross the finish line.

Leaders are only as successful as their teams and the great ones know that with the right team dynamics, decisions and diverse personalities, everyone wins in the end.

"*Coming together is a beginning, keeping together is a progress, and working together is success.*"
— **Henry Ford**

As John reviewed the article, he thought of the enormous importance of assembling and leading a mission-driven team. Until now, John focused his journey on his own skillset, but realized that, as his company grew, so would his team. He felt he'd enjoy leading a team, but already felt the substantial pressure that went along with it. John understood his vision and his values, but that was not enough. He'd be tasked with the responsibility of communicating those goals with a group of people that likely came from different backgrounds, had a variety of opinions and beliefs, and were just joining the fun, rather than creating a company from the ground up. The six lessons outlined in the Forbes article felt comfortable to John, and he related to the notion that, to truly succeed, he would need to build a team that truly bought in to his purpose and his goals.

In addition to the article, Sri provided John with a direct connect and introduction to Nicole Rodrigues. John did a little bit of research to prepare with his call with Nicole, and learned she was a former top model and a serial entrepreneur and the founder and CEO of Dubai-based Diva Group of Companies. She initiated her entrepreneurial journey with the launch of Diva Modeling and Events in 2003. After the phenomenal success of her modeling agency, the company branched out into real estate by starting Diva Holdings. In 2010, the company established NM Investments and further expanded its horizons by venturing into consulting and accounting services. By 2011, Nicole added two more business lines, Diva Laundry and Diva Salon. Nicole has been bestowed with several awards over the years. In 2015, she was recognized in the Outstanding Category at the Asia Pacific Entrepreneurship Awards. In 2014, Nicole was acknowledged as one of the Forbes Top Indian Leaders in the Arab World. She also won the CEO of the year at the CEO Awards in 2014. Today, the Diva Group of companies is capitalizing on its homegrown success and expanding its operations to Qatar, Kuwait, Doha, Bahrain, Turkey, India and Pakistan.

Sri suggested he review the Forbes article, while also learning a little bit more about Nicole before making contact. He reviewed both the article and Nicole's bio, just in time to find his phone ringing with an incoming call from outside the United States.

"Hello?" John said, a sense of eagerness in his voice.

"Please hold for Ms. Rodrigues."

The line went silent, followed by some upbeat dance music. After a few seconds, a calm and soothing voice came on the line.

"This is Nicole. Is this John?"

"Hey, Nicole. It is. Thank you so much for connecting with me. Sri had such nice things to say about you. I know you are busy, so I really appreciate your willingness to chat with me. I sent you a few questions to prep for our call. Were you able to review them?"

"Yes, John. No problem at all. The questions were great, and certainly touch on one of my favorite topics: building a winning team. That is one of my top priorities, and because my parent company has so many subsidiaries, we have incorporated a systematic way to build strong teams to lead our holdings. So, this is right in my wheelhouse."

John responded: "That is great. I looked at your site, and it looks like you are involved in a variety of different industries. However, I thought to myself how consistent your brand seemed, which I really liked. Even in all the different playing fields, your vision and brand remain clear. Was that important to you?"

"To me, passion is something that you can stay awake for, run miles for, sacrifice for and expect nothing back. Diva is an expression of my passion for everyone and everything beautiful. I love what I do, I love adding value and creating something that brings a smile to society. I want to provide a platform that is safe and secure for young talent. Fashion is my passion, and I respect the creativity that you find in its different levels. Whether you're trying to learn a new sport or trying to learn in life, I've always tried to be observant and learn more and evolve. My hope is that my vision trickles down to all my team members. But it starts with each of them seeing just how passionate I am.

"I work hard to nurture my team and create balance between give and take through giving everything you have consistently and continuously. I remind my team who they aim to be, and guide them to reach their own personal goals through the platform. We align goals, vision and a value system with respect for other humans. Diva is an institution that is focused on creating and innovating new ideas daily for better improvement of human capital. All of my team members buy into that. We do it through regular team meetings and one-on-one evaluations—reminders and reinforcements with accountability."

> *"Teamwork is the ability to work together toward a common vision. The ability to direct individual accomplishments toward organizational objectives. It is the fuel that allows common people to attain uncommon results."*
> — **Andrew Carnegie**

"It's so important that your management team is aligned on similar goals and not consumed with reinventing the wheel when not required. Candor is a basic rule for all. If you articulate a clear vision, a clear mission to help your team understand their roles in it, and then ask them to buy into the system, everyone will band together to make it happen."

John took a deep breath and responded, "I love it. You seem so mission-driven to succeed, and I appreciate that you instill your vision into all cracks and crevices of your business. That is surely not easy, especially with all of the expansion you've experienced. How have you worked to build and maintain a strong team?"

"Good question," Nicole said. "The building, training, grooming, mentoring and support of all team members runs rampant in our organizations. We hire energetic individuals that are interested in learning. Sugar, spice and everything nice is what I'd like to be made of, but I view myself as a true warrior princess. I am tough, strong, fearless, and hardworking. I'm not afraid to work, and I view myself as a solution-provider and not a problem-creator, fair and just so everyone benefits. When it comes to my team, I take a similar approach. I want tough, strong-willed and dedicated team members. My job is to implement a clear-cut vision supported by my personal values, and then it is the responsibility of the team we assembled to execute at a high level. If we have done our job and built a fantastic team, we will reach our scheduled goals."

"Thank you Nicole. That is fantastic insight. I love that you shared that with me. I know you have another call scheduled in just a couple minutes, so I wanted to part ways by asking you just one more question. Right now, I am focusing on building a business, but I know I will eventually have to create a team. Any specific steps to do that?"

"Yes. We use a four-step formula to build teams and accomplish goals:

1. Dream
2. Plan
3. Produce
4. Analyze

"Take those steps throughout the journey and you will find yourself with a team
that will make you proud. Thanks again for connecting. Off to my next call."

John responded, "Thanks Nicole. I hope to connect again soon."

John felt refreshed after his call with Nicole. It was strange to think that he would eventually lead a team, and the guidance Nicole offered would be remarkably helpful.

John decided, in that moment, that he would lead with these four pillars at the forefront of his mind, always using them as guiding lights in an otherwise difficult journey.

> *"Successful Teams struggle, fight and bicker, too. The difference between a Successful Team and a Failing Team: when these challenges happen, Successful Teams acknowledge and resolve them quickly because the vision, harmony, consistent production, and success of the team is more important than any 'he said/she said' drama or counterproductive foolishness."*
> **— Ty Howard**

CHAPTER 9:

LESSON #9: RIGHT PEOPLE, RIGHT PLACE & RIGHT TIME:

Goal Alignment Is the Key to Movement

"Get the right people on the bus, the wrong people off the bus, and the right people in the right seats."
— Jim Collins

As John leaned back in his oversized, black executive chair, he exhaled, staring out his floor to window ceilings that overlooked the beautiful downtown skyline. Just twelve months before, John emailed Sri and asked if they could chat for a few minutes. That led to meeting after meeting, interview after interview, and lesson after lesson. Over the past twelve months, John compiled an amazing group of mentors, people who he calls friends, and whose generosity has opened a remarkable set of doors.

John would never forget the day he took out a small business loan to rent some Class A office space, or recruiting and then hiring Sam, his right-hand man and first employee. In just the past year, Telos had grown from a one-man show to over ten employees. Together, his team of software engineers and salesman diligently worked to develop software for the educational industry, now creating a product that could link those in need of education with those that could provide it through modern day technology. John's company manufactured the software, but also hired the teachers, produced the course curriculum, and generated interactive software that could deliver education through students via iPads and other tablets.

In just the first few months, John rolled out his product to just a few underdeveloped countries. But now, John found his software was being used to offer education programs in over 75 countries. His growth was exponential, and he attracted numerous angel investors. Telos had truly arrived, when, in the past 30 days, they completed their first round of funding, raising over 5 million dollars for future software development and the marketing of its products.

John couldn't be happier with the progress of Telos. But even more importantly, he was content within his own professional and personal life. It wasn't easy to turn his back on a high-paying, six-figure job, and all the security that goes along with it. But he followed his heart, and it paid off greatly. John was now the CEO of a multi-million-dollar technology company. He couldn't believe it: corner office, beautiful space, ten employees, and a vision for the future. John was on top of the world. He had to pinch himself on a regular basis, to be sure that he wasn't dreaming.

As he surveyed his walls, he reviewed each of the pictures affixed to the sheet-rock. Picture after picture of John and the people that helped him along the way. Over the past year, John developed relationships with new friends, many of whom he met through Sri and the HBS portal. He couldn't have ever imagined just how close-knit and generous his mentors were with their time. Even though many of them ran large and successful companies, they were all willing to step away from their busy lives and offer John just a few minutes of their time. That investment led to remarkable returns for John. He knew he'd never reach this point on his own, and couldn't feel more appreciation for the gifts each of these people offered him.

As Telos grew, John recognized many of the same growing pains any new business struggles with—hiring the right team, implementing a direct mission, executing a vision, and creating a culture that supports exciting growth and development. John spent the better part of the past year to ensure his business was one to be modeled after, constantly taking survey of where they were and exactly where they were heading. With these new responsibilities, John quickly realized he had no choice but to delegate many of the day-to-day operations to his team. John built this not-so-little company from the ground up. He started it from his small office, and scaled it and expanded it into being a substantial business offering a product that could literally change the world.

Now, John faced an entirely new challenge, which he planned to welcome with open arms: with the influx of cash, John was now able to hire a full sales team, and had thirty days to interview and secure five brand new employees to take Telos to the next level. The projected sales for the forthcoming year were over 10 million, so he realized each new team member would be responsible for at least 2 million dollars in new accounts. While that sounded like a daunting number, John knew he would hit his target if he hired the right people.

> *"Just as your car runs more smoothly and requires less energy to go faster and farther when the wheels are in perfect alignment, you perform better when your thoughts, feelings, emotions, goals, and values are in balance."*
> — **Brian Tracy**

Before John began accepting resumes, he decided to reach out to Sri in hopes that Sri could offer some crucial feedback on the best practices for hiring. During their conversation, Sri reminded John that aligning your goals with your team members' purpose is the quickest way to achieve positive outcomes. Take the right people, at the right place, at the right time, and then sprinkle in goal alignment, and you notice your business take off like a rocket ship. In their conversation, Sri referenced a Cornell University article, written by Christopher Collins, Jeff Ericksen, and Matthew Allen.

The article, entitled, *Human Resource Management Practices, Workforce Alignment, and Firm Performance*[5], stated:

> *"Do people contribute to the success of small businesses? When addressing this question, it is necessary to point out that the strategic human resource goal of any small business is workforce alignment. A company with an aligned workforce has (a) the right types of people, (b) in the right places at the right times, (c) doing the right things right. A company with the right types of people has employees with the knowledge and skills necessary to help the firm achieve its goals. A company with people in the right places at the right times effectively utilizes its people and, thus, gets the most out of its employees' knowledge and skills. Finally, a company with people doing*

5   http://digitalcommons.ilr.cornell.edu/cgi/viewcontent. cgi?article=1004&context=cahrswp

the right things right has employees that always act in ways that help the company succeed. The three components of workforce alignment are highly interrelated. It is tough, for example, for people to act in ways that foster firm success if they do not possess the knowledge and skills necessary to do so or if they are mismanaged (i.e., in the wrong places at the wrong times). In short, then, when all three components are present, then there is workforce alignment and this, in turn, should help drive company success.

The results of the study are presented as follows:

First, we provide a visual depiction of the study's findings.

Second, we show that workforce alignment is strongly related to small business success.

Third, we demonstrate how various employee selection, management, and motivation strategies affect workforce alignment. Fourth, we present four key takeaways from the study.

Finally, we provide a section that allows you to compare your company's results on all study variables to those of the other 250 companies that participated in the study.

Overview of Study Results

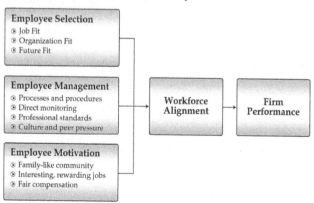

The article continued by outlining the four key takeaways for managers interested in improving the performance of their small businesses. These include:

5. _Don't forget about people_. Companies with well-aligned workforces outperform companies with less aligned workforces on seven key indicators of performance. When looking for ways to improve company performance, don't forget about people management strategies!

6. _Keep an eye on the future when hiring_. When hiring new people, most companies seek to match people to specific jobs. The results of this study suggest that this type of focus does not help create workforce alignment. Instead, companies should seek to hire new people capable of making a positive, long-term contribution to the firm.

7. _Manage employees through formal processes and procedures or professional standards_. In small businesses, it is easy for managers to make the mistake of constantly looking over the shoulders of employees. The results of this study suggest that this is a poor way to achieve workforce alignment. Instead, companies benefit from either developing formal management systems or providing employees the opportunity to manage themselves.

8. _A family-like community is a powerful way to motivate employees_. Many scholars and managers assume that compensation is the best way to motivate people. The results of this study, in contrast, suggest that workforce alignment is best achieved by developing a family-like sense of community.

John considered these four pillars, and recognized they'd be extremely important as he worked to assemble a sales team and to create an environment where his goals were directly aligned with theirs. It seemed unlikely anyone would carry the same driven passion towards the educational software Telos produced, but John wanted to find people that felt strongly about the service or product they offered to the consumer or to other business professionals. The best he could do was focus on employee engagement and alignment to ensure he accomplished that goal.

"It doesn't make sense to hire smart people and tell them what to do; we hire smart people so they can tell us what to do"
— **Steve Jobs**

Along with this article, Sri offered John one last parting gift — an introduction to a close friend, Andre Kissajikian. John did some initial research before their scheduled call. He learned that Andre is the founder and CEO of AK Reality, a residential and commercial real estate company. He managed over a multi-million dollars' worth of real estate, and had a reputation for being a well-respected and passionate businessman. John dialed his number, right at their scheduled conference time, and Andre picked up the phone.

"Hello, John — how are you?"

John immediately noticed Andre's Brazilian accent. "Fine. Thank you so much for connecting with me. I am really at an exciting crossroads in my business. Sri told me you'd be the perfect guy to chat with. Mind if I fill you in?"

"Sure. Of course. Tell me how I can help."

John then brought Andre up to speed, recapping his growth and discussing the past twelve months of his business. After a few minutes of outline, John then posed the following question: "Andre — I now stand at the foot of a very important decision. We are about to hire a sales team, and I am extremely sensitive to the notion that I am proud of my company and confident of our goals. But I always wonder if I can instill that same pride and goal alignment within my team. I am not sure I can. As your business grew, was that a concern for you?"

"John, I understand passion as the intense enthusiasm and deep commitment to your company, your work, and your future perspectives. I believe that passion is inherent to effective leaders, and I relate it to my commitment and responsibilities as a leader, aligning the strategic conditions of its evolution with a vision of my company. To lead a differentiated, competitive, and institutionalized company, with sustainable growth, makes me proud and passionate, stimulating me to assume a posture of profound involvement. I bet you feel the same way."

"Absolutely. I do."

"Well then, in a modern, competitive organization, it seems to me essential to have a purpose and cause. On a personal level, I have clarity around the importance and the contribution of various stakeholders — employees, customers, suppliers, partners, communities in which we operate — for our performance and future prospects. Our cause/purpose reveals the commitment to contribute to public trust and the construction of shared perspectives that generate healthy results. Truly, our stakeholders and participants are linked to the purpose of our activities in order to achieve mutual benefit. There is an intimate relationship between my personal and business values. These core values are manifested in our strategic modeling, including high ethical standards, excellence, and respect, enhancing the client concept, governance, participatory management, etc. More than a formal record, these are the values that I seek to put in practice and express conscious and mature beliefs."

"That makes perfect sense," John responded. "I think you have to start on a personal level before you can align with your ultimate goals on a professional level. Just like you, I worked hard to ensure I had personal clarity. My hope (and biggest concern) is that I can now implement that in a newly hired sales team."

"Yup — that's it. I have a goal to develop my team continuously, observing seven priority aspects. These include:

1. Ethics
2. Maturity
3. Academic training
4. Constructive attitude
5. Excellence
6. Effectiveness/outcomes
7. Commitment

I witness the alignment and evolution of my team regarding these aspects, producing consistent conditions for performance and a sustainable and solid business. This process observes the competitive market, context, and the environment of my company, the individual approach, and the collective approach.

To have the right people in the right places is of the utmost importance, and you have to consider these seven traits. Additionally, we must align these premises, with a background of prospective and strategic direction, to carry out the performance in a consistent and consequent manner. That is, although a necessary premise, you must articulate with the environments and strategic definitions. Then, and perhaps only then, can you ensure you are moving in the right direction.

I always love referencing Jim Collins' *Good to Great*. You have to get the right people on the bus. Get the right people on the bus, the wrong people off the bus, and the right people in the right seats. Jim

Collins' quote from *Good to Great* is now famous, and powerful in its simplicity and logic — yet it is not easy to accomplish. Just how do successful entrepreneurs find the right people and keep them on the bus? I would suggest the following:

- ☐ The right people have personal values that closely align with a company's core values. They can articulate these values and are willing to promote and spread them to others.
- ☐ The right people do not have to be tightly managed. They expect delegation, and don't thrive in a control-oriented hierarchy.
- ☐ The right people understand they don't have a job; they have a responsibility to achieve results. When you fly, do you want the air traffic controller to have a job directing airplanes, or a responsibility to land planes safely?
- ☐ The right people do what they say they will do and want to be held accountable for results. They are careful about what they commit to and deliver 100% on their commitments.
- ☐ The right people practice "window/mirror thinking." When things go well they are transparent, pointing out success factors in others and not taking all the glory. When things don't go well, the glass window becomes a mirror they face, and take responsibility.
- ☐ The right people have a real passion for the company and the work it does."

John said, "That's great advice. I am going to implement those seven traits in my hiring and implementation of goal alignments. I really appreciate your insight. Would you mind if I follow up with you if necessary?"

"Of course. Thanks so much for reaching out. Let me know how I can help you. Ciao, my friend."

"An intelligent person hires people who are more intelligent than he is."
— **Robert Kiyosaki**

John took out a large legal pad and black pen from his desk drawer. He drew a number of horizontal and vertical lines on it, creating seven boxes. On the top, he wrote the following:

- *Name:*
- *References:*
- *Current Job:*
- *Grade:*

He then followed these specifics with the seven traits Andre had shared with him. His intention was to create a form, which would assist in his interviews. Since posting the open position on social media, John had received over 200 applications. With the help of Sam, he whittled it down to the thirty most eligible candidates, and scheduled interviews with each of them. He was determined to meet directly with each one, to ensure that they jived and what was their specific goal alignment. With the help of this newly created document, John knew he could easily determine the real fabric of each candidate.

"Successful people maintain a positive focus in life no matter what is going on around them. They stay focused on their

> *past successes rather than their past failures, and on the*
> *next action steps they need to take to get them closer to the*
> *fulfillment of their goals rather than all the other distractions*
> *that life presents to them."*
> **— Jack Canfield**

John felt confident that if he could find applicants who were ethical, mature, committed, academics, with a positive attitude towards excellence, that he would be in good shape. After filling in the last few traits, he ran off thirty copies and wrote the name of each applicant on top. He then buzzed his secretary, Sydney, and indicated that he was ready to meet with the first candidate.

CHAPTER 10:

LESSON #10: EMPOWERING GROWTH:

Lead, Manage, Delegate

*"Strength and growth come only through continuous effort
and struggle."*
— **Napoleon Hill**

Remaining focused on building his team, John was able to hire five new salespeople in just under thirty days. He enjoyed the interview process, but found it difficult to choose the best candidates. However, he constantly assessed and evaluated each team member using those skills Andre shared with him. Six months had elapsed since his new team joined the fun, and they seemed to be progressing accordingly. It had been just sixty days since John released them to sell their products, and Telos recognized substantial growth within those first two months. It was beyond John's wildest dreams. He hadn't expected this much this soon, but reveled in the excitement that came along with it. John realized that this was just a taste and there was more to come.

Throughout his educational journey, John learned the importance of empowering growth. However, it was not always easy to apply those qualities to the real world. Even with an expanding team, John still found himself working 15+ hour days, and taking responsibility for much of the company sales. He just couldn't fully delegate tasks, and, while Telos kept humming along and selling, John noticed leaking within his company. Some of the products were not delivered on time, others were riddled with programming glitches, and there were extensive consumer complaints regarding the customer support for the products. In short, John was not delegating enough to his sales team, and in turn, other areas of his business suffered.

It was clear to John that growth expanded revenue, but it also introduced greater responsibility into the business. They go hand-in-hand. John decided he needed to be much more self-aware. He was spending time in the wrong places, and needed to shift his attention to the problems in his company, rather than just putting his head down mostly on selling.

"Without continual growth and progress, such words as 'improvement, achievement, and success' have no meaning."
— **Benjamin Franklin**

John's decision to make a change led him to a meeting with Arieh Ruzansky, a close friend of Sri's. Sri sent John a link to Arieh's

LinkedIn page, and John learned that Arieh began his company in Mexico City. His background was in industrial engineering. During his second year in college, Mexico City opened up to international trade. Arieh's response was to travel to China to determine if there were any lucrative business opportunities there. He traveled to Hong Kong, and started to import ladies' handbags, and that is how he started his business. At the time, Arieh and his family were the first importers in Mexico City.

It took Arieh only four years to truly succeed. But competition was stiff, and many people started importing as well. To differentiate himself, Arieh approached Disney, and after a year of tough negotiations, received the rights to license Disney in Mexico City, a true differentiator. It was that backdrop and information that Sri shared with John before connecting him with Arieh. John was excited to connect with Arieh, as John was currently struggling with scaling his own company. He was hopeful their call would help John empower growth.

"This is Arieh."

" Hi Arieh — this is John. Thanks so much for connecting with me. I really appreciate it. Sri spoke highly of you and thinks you'd be a great guiding light for my journey."

"No problem, John. I actually spoke with Sri last night, and he shared your story with me. It is very impressive you decided to give up the traditional job you had to follow your dream. I did something very similar when I was a young guy. It really ended up paying off. The risk was substantial, but I felt I saw an opportunity to enter the marketplace and make a difference."

"Exactly," John said. "I was happy in my former profession, but I was not fulfilled. I did not feel great purpose and it kind of seemed like I was just floating away, getting by."

"I can understand the feeling. It is not easy. I remain extremely satisfied with my business. I still cannot believe how it has grown. We were the first Mexican company to enter into the U.S. with Disney and service the Hispanic market. That was almost 15 years ago, and we started with no sales and one employee. Today, we are around $100 million in sales and have over 400 employees. We have subsidiaries in the U.S., Puerto Rico, and Central America, Brazil, China, and the Caribbean."

"Very impressive. It sounds like you have scaled your company considerably. I am not nearly at that size, but my company, Telos, is starting to experience substantial growth and I am finding my leadership style and delegation ability is not servicing us as well as I would like. I want to be hands-on, but I recognize I need to do more than sell. I have to manage the big picture and focus on growth, not a sale here and a sale there."

Arieh responded. "That is a common problem. I think we all feel that way. My leadership style is definitely team-oriented. I work very close to the team, but I also realize how important it is to have smart people around you, so they can run the show. Remember three things:

1. Lead
2. Manage
3. Delegate

You cannot be everything to everyone. You have to remain supportive and be a good listener, so you are aware of what is going on in your business. But you just cannot do it all. I have always considered myself more strategic than operational. I still spend about 70% of my time coaching my team, listening to them, and solving problems and challenges together. And I recognize that I am a perfectionist, so there are times when I overstep my boundaries. But, I work to roll out a five-year plan, and then set it into action. We put the target as far away as possible, while still remaining extremely reachable. It will never be easy to delegate. This is your baby. However, if you want to recognize extreme growth, you'll have no choice but to determine what you can do, and what you don't need to do."

> *"Lead from the back & let others believe they are in the front."*
> **— Nelson Mandela**

John responded: "I totally get it. But boy is that easier said than done."

Arieh said, "You have to hire a great team — one you trust. We look at four qualities when making hiring decisions. We want people that have:

1. Strong values
2. A good attitude
3. Very knowledgeable
4. Extremely experienced

"We are in good shape if we can check those four boxes. We then have to lead those new employees by managing them and teaching them. I have five people that report directly to me. Each of those is a leader with 15 years of experience within my company. We have a training program within the company because every time we doubled the business, the skills the people needed to succeed became much more complex. We always want to elevate our team members and prepare them to advance within the company. We pay for education, higher learning and even additional scholastic endeavors, like MBAs.

"I guess it's a matter of continuously learning — it's a learning process. Sometimes you need outside skills, but most of it comes from the inside."

"That makes sense. Even then, it is not always easy to just let go. I trust my team fully, but I still want to have my hand in a little bit of everything, whether it is good for me and Telos or not."

> *"If you pick the right people and give them the opportunity to spread their wings and put compensation as a career behind it you almost don't have to manage them."*
> **— Jack Welch**

Arieh said, "I understand. That is completely natural. As leaders, we both have a certain type of personality. But…that desire to have your hand in everything will actually stifle your growth in the long run. But you have to remember to lead, manage, and delegate. The third part is often the most difficult — but it also positions you in the greatest position for success. For example, we have a conference every four months. The entire company comes together, and I speak to them about where we are going and discuss our forthcoming goals. I find it much easier to present the goals, rather than attempt to achieve each one on my own. If I can constantly remind my team of our targets, we can always work to make them a reality. It comes down to direct communication, and empowering your entire company to hit the target.

"We could have a conference call, or a webinar, but I want everyone in the same auditorium, collaborating and excited about what's to come. When we come together, you can feel the energy. And that is a time where I have the opportunity to lead, to manage, and then to empower my team by delegating responsibility. We value teamwork and work to put our money where our mouth is. In fact, we are #38 on the list for the Top 100 Companies to Work for in the Country. I take great pride in that. The reality is the best way to empower your team is by giving them REAL responsibility — by showing them trust through creating high expectations for them. It is not always easy, especially when you are skilled and trained to accomplish some of these goals."

John responded: "That is remarkable. Now that I think of it, I would really like to work to gain similar recognition. I really want to build a place where people strive to work. I want my employees to be supported and excited about coming to work. The reason companies like Google and Zappos are successful is because of their team. And the reason they have such a great team is because they attract the best of the best. It really makes perfect sense."

Arieh continued. "That is how I feel. It is so much easier to delegate and focus on new ways to grow when you are confident you have a strong team. Growth is a unique concept. You built what you built, and you started the growth potential. But now, if you do not step aside to some degree, and focus on a different kind of growth, you'll actually limit your ability to scale. It isn't easy, but you have to realize you cannot do this alone."

John said, "I always reference Michael Jordan's quote: 'Talent wins games, but teamwork and intelligence wins championships.' That really hits close to home. I realize that I worked hard to scale my company, and I then decided part of that growth was to hire a talented team. If I am to grow from a 1-million-dollar business to a 100 million dollar business, I have to take a step back, and recognize what I can do, and what I have no need to do. I think of myself as a smart guy, but I am squeezing my company. Gosh Arieh, you really put me in a position to do a little self-evaluation. I cannot thank you enough. Would it be ok if I contacted you in the near future with any further questions?"

"Of course, John. Any friend of Sri's is a friend of mine. The truth of it is that you will get there. It may not be easy, but realize you are walking the same path as many entrepreneurs that came before you. We all deal with the inner-conflict created by empowering growth. On one hand, you want to be selfish, keeping your baby close to your heart. But on the other hand, you have to release some of the control you have over it for it to truly recognize how far it can go. Take a deep breath, and remember:

1. Lead
2. Manage
3. Delegate

> *"If you really want to grow as an entrepreneur, you've got to learn to delegate."*
> — **Sir Richard Branson**

John knew he had to focus his efforts on his management style, shifting away from the day-to-day operations, and focus more energy on empowering growth. So, he took out a large legal pad, in hopes of solving this continued issue. He decided to create a chart, with the following headers:

Lead, Manage, and Delegation Assessment

Things I can delegate:

_____

_____

_____

_____

_____

_____

Things I cannot delegate:

_____

_____

_____

_____

_____

Is this task one I often see within my business? If so, set aside time for adequate training before delegating.

_____

_____

_____

_____

_____

_____

Delegate the responsibilities and agree on expectations:

_____

_____

_____

_____

_____

_____

Schedule follow-ups on the delegated tasks & monitor progress (Manage):

_____

_____

_____

_____

_____

_____

Grow leaders within by providing continuous learning opportunities (Lead):

_____

_____

_____

_____

_____

_____

"As all entrepreneurs know, you live and die by your ability to prioritize. You must focus on the most important, mission-critical tasks each day and night, and then share, delegate, delay or skip the rest."
— Jessica Jackley

As John filled in his newly created questionnaire, he began to realize just how hands-on he had become. He didn't feel remorse for his tendencies, as he recognized this helped to position Telos in the marketplace. But he knew that, as his company grew, he would have to trust his team members to get the job done. He felt a sense of calmness, knowing that he spent a great deal of effort to hire the best team possible. John looked at the clock in his office, surprised to find it was after 9:00 p.m., and he was hungry. He smiled, shrugged, and appreciated this was just another example of exactly why he needed to shift some of his responsibilities to those he entrusted with his business.

CHAPTER 11:

LESSON #11: THE 4 P'S OF SUCCESS:

Precision, Planning, Prioritization & Perseverance

"Plans are nothing; planning is everything."
— Dwight Eisenhower

After almost two years of operating, John felt comfortable in the direction of his business. Over the past 24 months, Telos saw a number of ups and downs, but through it all, John and his company were not just surviving but truly thriving. John felt a sense of pride in his business, knowing he followed his passion and it was starting to truly pay off. He almost laughed at the thought of remaining in his previous job, unhappy and unfulfilled. He truly loved waking up and driving to his office. He was finally fulfilling his life's purpose, and couldn't get enough. Growth was not always easy, but he had become better at delegated responsibilities and refined his day-to-day activities to be less hands on in the sales department and more focused on scaling the business. Once he was finally able to let go, he realized a sense of calmness, one he thought wouldn't ever exist.

That shift in his efforts resulted in remarkable growth. In the past twelve months alone, Telos's revenue doubled many times over. For the first time, John decided to take a salary and was able to invest in a new home on the east side of the city. He didn't know what to do with all the extra room in his home. Six months after purchasing it, he had furniture in only one room. But he was happy, and really enjoyed his new life. John took it one day at a time and did his best to enjoy the ride.

It was 12:30 p.m., and John had just finished a quick lunch at his desk. He ate his usual: a green salad with chicken on it with an iced coffee. As he was throwing away the remnants of his lunch, he heard Sherri's voice over his intercom.

"John — I have the Vice President of Learning, Inc. on the phone. He says it is extremely important and needs to chat as soon as possible."

"You can send him through," John responded, sensing something was wrong and feeling a pit in his stomach.

"Dan, hello. What's going on?"

"Hey John. Hope things are going well. I am sorry for the urgency of the call, but we have an issue. We implemented your new science and math technology into over 500 schools nationwide in the past two weeks. The thing is, we have received almost simultaneous reports that the software had extensive bugs in it. Those bugs ended up crashing over 6,000 computers. Gone. All the data. All the information. School records. Lesson plans. The schools are upset. They are spending thousands of dollars trying to recover from this catastrophe. We are doing everything we can to assist them, but we are spending way too much and don't have the manpower necessary to help with a full recovery. My guess is we lose them all as clients, which will cost us about 5 million dollars in annual revenue."

John felt sick to his stomach. Over the past two years, John had worked closely in developing the software. This seemed to be impossible. He couldn't understand how this occurred. Regardless, he now had to deal with it.

"Dan, I am so sorry. I am shocked by this news. What can I do to help you?"

"Well, we first have to get your people at these sites and review the software to see if we can resolve this issue. The schools understand things like this can happen. But that doesn't mean they are happy about it. To be frank, I think we can all recover from this, but I am not sure we can continue to do business with Telos. This is one of those situations where we have no choice but to point fingers just to save our own ass. I hate the idea that we couldn't work together, but this is a big deal. I have known you for over a year, and I really enjoy our time on the golf course, but I just can't take this one on the chin. No one saw this coming. But we now have to figure out how the heck to fix it."

"I feel sick, Dan. I cannot apologize enough. Doing business together is not my concern at this moment. I want to see what I can do to help fix this situation. I have ten software engineers I can deploy at the drop of a hat. I can likely source another ten immediately through a recruiter. I know that isn't much, but they should be able to remotely connect to the computers and determine what happened. Once we figure that out, we can create a software update and send it to every school electronically. They can then update the software, which will hopefully remedy the problem, without any more loss. I am just so terribly sorry this occurred."

Dan quickly responded with a tone of annoyance, "John, it is what it is. This sort of thing happens. We just need to fix this, and then figure out where to go from here. Call me before close of business with an update. I have to go and chat with the shareholders."

John heard the line click and go dead. He couldn't believe his ears. Telos developed great software. It was the backbone of the business, and John invested a large sum of money in hiring the most proficient software engineers. This felt like a nightmare, and John still couldn't believe this occurred. As he continued to process the information provided by Dan, he started to play out scenarios in his head.

Even if he resolved the issue in the forthcoming days, he knew his relationship with Learning, Inc. was at risk. John understood politics as well as the next guy, and someone had to take the fall for this. It made perfect sense for Learning, Inc. to point the finger at Telos, and John expected that to be the case. Although just an estimate, John guessed his relationship with Learning, Inc. comprised about 22% of the previous year's revenue. Losing a client like Learning, Inc. could be catastrophic. John closed his eyes, sighed deeply, and began to click away at his computer, looking, maybe even praying for an answer.

> *"All the adversity I've had in my life, all my troubles and obstacles, have strengthened me. You may not realize it when it happens, but a kick in the teeth may be the best thing in the world for you."*
> — **Walt Disney**

John had planned for a day like this. Well, not exactly. However, he knew there would be obstacles along the way, and he recognized that he'd likely be tested to the fabric of his core. Telos survived through it all, and John knew how to steer the ship through torrential waters. But this was nothing like he ever imagined. This was catastrophic. John was about to lose his largest client, and felt terrible that his software caused so many problems for these schools. The goal of Telos was to help children learn, and his software just knocked out over 6,000 computers that assist in this goal. Over the past few days, John deployed his team of software engineers, even coming out of pocket to hire ten more. They had yet to develop a resolution, but one by one they were remotely logging into the infected computers and working to recover the lost data.

His team helped to recover one computer every 15 — 20 minutes, and John estimated it would take two weeks of around the clock work to remedy the crashed computers. On top of that, they had to figure out the reason for the failed software, develop a solution, and then install it on each computer. There was no timeframe for that, as it could take days, weeks, or months. John hadn't slept in three days, and he was close to a breaking point. He was at his wits' end. He spoke with Dan on what seemed like an hourly basis, and while Dan remained patient, he could sense the enormous stress and anxiety Dan was under as well. They were in the trenches together, and had to manage the situation before they could even survey the carnage caused by it.

In the meantime, John needed a break. He threw on the pair of shorts and running shoes he kept in his office closet, and took the elevator down to the ground floor. It was a beautiful spring day, and John felt as if he hadn't left the office in days. He exited the large double doors and stepped onto the sidewalk, surveying the crowd and taking a deep breath of fresh air. John then took off running. He ran fast, pushing himself, and trying to forget about his present situation. He looped the block five times, and, drenched in sweat, made it back to the front of the building. John felt relieved, as if he left some of his extensive stress behind him, somewhere on the streets. Just as he began to stretch, his phone rang. He noticed it was Sri. He smiled, happy to see the name of an old friend.

"Sri, hey. Thanks for calling me back. It is good to hear from you. I have had quite a run. I am sure you read my email, so you know what's been going on."

"Hey John. I did. I am sorry you are dealing with this. It sounds terrible, but you are doing what you need to do. Just keep putting one foot in front of another. You will get through this."

Feeling deflated, John responded, "I am sure I will, one way or another. But still, even then, I feel like I am drowning. It seems like there is no end in sight. And even if we recover and fix the computers, I am at risk of losing a huge customer. Even in a best case scenario, this really stinks."

"I understand. But you know this is part of it all. No business has ever dodged every bullet. How you handle this situation and recover from it will define you. Winston Churchill said, "Success is not final, failure is not fatal: it is the courage to continue that counts." So no matter what happens, it is not forever. But let me ask you this question — how did this happen? Have you assessed what caused this to occur?"

John sighed.

"To some degree. We aren't totally sure, but I think the issue boils down to the algorithm that processes answers and generates scores. We must have been off a few digits. We just weren't precise enough. That resulted in a chain reaction which basically caused the software to implode, taking everything along with it."

"Be precise. A lack of precision is dangerous when the margin of error is small."
Donald Rumsfeld

"It happens. You know as well as I do that when it comes to software, precision is key. You have to plan for every feasible outcome, even the most serious ones. No one wants to think his or her software will crash, but it certainly can. So you have to have a contingency plan in place. Have you evaluated versus the 4 P's of Success?"

"No. I have not. What are they?"

"Well, they seem quite relevant for your present situation. The 4 P's of Success are:

1. *Precision*
2. *Planning*
3. *Prioritization*
4. *Perseverance*

"Think about each one of these for a second. I am sure you are familiar with these terms, but in your present circumstances, let's unpack each one. It may help you to gain meaningful insight into finding a solution. To start, precision has failed you. Your algorithm is off. Some of the adjustments were wrong. Precision is an interesting word. Precision is a word that comes from two Latin words—*prae*, before, and *caedere*, to cut.

"So, an extension of this is that before you actually cut something, you should measure it and measure it and measure it. That is likely where the planning comes in. Plan to cut. Plan to measure. Plan for incorrect measurements. Plan for poor cutting, or execution. No matter what, precision and planning go hand-in-hand. You cannot be precise unless you plan to be precise. And your planning will fail if you were not precise in how you planned. Somewhere along the way, you just didn't plan to be precise enough. Don't take it personally — software fails all the time. That's just part of the game we play. You are talking about thousands and thousands of numerical values, taken out to the hundredth decimal. It is a ticking time bomb, a recipe for disaster."

John responded, "I know. And I realize that. But I really thought we were precise in our estimates. We planned this technology for over two years. It is not like it was developed overnight in a woodshed. We are talking about some of the best software engineers in the world."

"I know," Sri said. "Which shows just how difficult this can be. Even with the best, you can still royally mess it up. But that just shows you focused on the third "P", which is prioritization. You prioritized precision, and did it through a willingness to invest in the best engineers you could find. Imagine how bad this could be if you didn't have those engineers to help you solve this problem. Then where would you be? If you have a chance at salvaging this whole thing and maintaining a relationship with Learning, Inc., then it will be through how you responded to the situation, which is indicative of your priorities. Fix first; figure out the rest later. And the only way you can do that is through maintaining substantial perseverance, which is the final "P" of success. The most successful people in the world overcome all the obstacles in their paths. You will persevere through this. You have no choice. You aren't going to just crawl into a hole and allow Telos to die, are you?"

"Of course not. I am going to figure it out. I just don't know how."

"That is ok. You don't have to. You just have to know you want to. To this point, you demonstrate the 4 "P's" of success. Don't you realize that? You were precise, just not precise enough. You planned accordingly, and did all you could to implement an infrastructure you thought would work. And now, you are prioritizing a solution over money, and you are fighting through this mess. John, you are succeeding. You just may not realize it at the time."

"Thanks Sri. I needed the pep talk. But even then, this could end up costing us a lot more than money. It may cost us our reputation, our relationships, and most importantly, our ability to help children obtain education."

"You are right, John. It could. But I have a hunch that it won't. You are a survivor. And you haven't gotten where you are today because you aren't successful. Just remember: be precise, plan accordingly, prioritize what's important, and persevere through it all. Check your email, I just made an introduction to a friend I think could help you through this even better than I can."

> *"I do not think that there is any other quality so essential to success of any kind as the quality of perseverance. It overcomes almost everything, even nature."*
> — **John D. Rockefeller**

John checked his email and saw the following from Sri:

Christo,

Please meet John. He is a close friend and is in need of some guidance. Please connect and offer him some insight to the best of your ability. We had a nice conversation about the 4 P's of Success, and I thought you could help John further develop some ideas surrounding this concept. You were the first person to come to mind. I hope you and your family are doing great.

Thanks,

Sri

John felt a sense of relief upon seeing this email from Sri. Over the past two years, Sri has been an enormous mentor to John. He has offered an endless amount of education and care for John and his progress through the business world. It almost seemed as if Sri were one part mentor, one part shepherd, and one part savior. He was always there for John and often offered him guidance when he needed it the most. And now, more than ever, John needed it. John opened up a new search window and typed in Christo Angelkov's name. After a few clicks, he was staring at a picture of his future mentor, CEO of Iris Consulting in Bulgaria, a company that focuses on using information management to innovate and optimize business processes.

An exchange of emails ensued, and John scheduled a call with Christo for the next day.

John heard the crackle of Christo picking up the phone. His thick accent boomed through the receiver.

"John — Sri spoke highly of you and shared much about your company. I am excited to speak with you."

John responded, "I really appreciate your willingness to help me solve the problems my company is facing. Sri thought you'd be the perfect person to speak to about success. I was chatting with Sri, and we started to discuss business execution, and the conversation turned to what I call The 4 P's of Success. Those include precision, planning, prioritization and perseverance. I firmly believe that if you possess each of these traits, you can become a remarkable businessman."

Christo's voice perked up. "There is nothing more important than planning. Leadership, at any level, certainly isn't easy, but to manage exponential growth through proper planning is undoubtedly one of the biggest challenges in business. We don't espouse dozens of cliché-infused declarations such as "Let's focus on the key priorities this quarter," or "Customers come first," or "We need a full-court press in engineering this month." By doing that, precious time is wasted, talented people lose their focus, and big projects fail. We really don't need that. Without clear definitions and directions from the top, the team works ineffectively and at cross-purposes. In my experience, there are five topics that control the direction of the train. These include:

1. Organizational Structure and Hierarchy
2. Financial Results
3. A Leader's Sense of His or Her Job
4. Time Management
5. Corporate Culture

"Each one is important in its own way. For example:

1. ***Organizational structure and hierarchy.*** Because it represents individual power or influence, hierarchy is an emotionally-charged framework even during a company's most stable times. If a CEO fails to take definitional control of a reorganization, with its prospect of job losses, boss changes, and new modes of working, the whole company can grind to a halt. If you multiply that time by employee salaries, and factor in the inevitable lapses in customer service and product innovation during the period, you can conservatively estimate the damage to the company. The most productive way for a leader to think about organizational structure is as a flexible map of accountability for action and, thus, results — a guideline whose purpose is to define goals and optimize resources, not to oust or devalue employees.

2. ***Financial Results.*** "Results" is another powerful concept that, left unmanaged, poses a risk to a company's long-term health. Effective leaders understand that there is more

leverage in using quarterly results as a metric for long-term improvement than in worrying only about short-term market wins. By using results as a diagnostic tool in the service of improving future execution, and by asking employees to participate in the analysis, effective leaders encourage honesty and engage their troops in open dialogue. Employees are more likely to generate good ideas, and the firm is more likely to surpass financial expectations quarter after quarter.

3. *A Leader's Sense of His or Her Job.* CEOs wear many hats and play many roles in the service of leadership. However, surrounded by people who seek their feedback and approval, some fall into the trap of thinking that their responsibility is to be the person who has all the answers. Effective leaders, by contrast, understand that their role is to bring out the answers in others. They do this by very clearly and explicitly seeking contributions, challenges, and collaboration from the people who report to them, using their positional power not to dominate but rather to drive the decision-making process. The more collaborative and apolitical that process is, the less isolated the leader, and the greater the likelihood that the business strategy will be grounded in reality.

4. *Time management.* Every executive feels that time is in short supply. Organizers, time management classes, and administrative assistants remind us of the time we don't have. Obsessed with deadlines, managers struggle against constraints by trying to squeeze, manipulate, and control the limited hours in the day. When the CEO gives employees the message that time is the boss, the "to-do list" mentality can easily subsume important goals. Instead of struggling against time, my choices are within the time constraint. How could my people best use their hours? Instead of playing 'beat the

clock' by trying to do everything I wished, where could they best focus their energy? How could time be optimized? By understanding that I have a choice about how the limited time could best be used, I am able to free up needed technical and marketing resources and focus on quality and branding.

"The key is not to prioritize what's on your schedule, but to schedule your priorities."
— Stephen Covey

5. ***Corporate Culture.*** Culture is not created by declaration; it derives from expectations focused on winning. You can only have a culture that encourages performance if you hire the right people, require them to behave in a way that is consistent with the values the company espouses, and implement processes that will allow the company to win in the marketplace. A healthy culture is created and maintained by focusing on the right goals and creating the experience of winning in the marketplace.

"I've come to the conclusion that the real job of leadership is to inspire the organization to take responsibility for creating a better future. That occurs through The 4 P's of Success, often discussed and referenced by authors Jim Kouzes and Barry Posner. I believe effective communication is a leader's single most critical management tool for making this happen. I've accepted that the leader's job, at its core, is to inspire and support the organization's collective responsibility to create better potentialities for the company. Good communication, between the various departments of the team, underlies it."

John heard Christo exhale. "That is fantastic advice. Has perseverance played a role in your successful entrepreneurial career? What is your advice to upcoming entrepreneurs?"

"Perseverance is not merely a good business principle — it is imperative for a successful and lasting career. As Steve Jobs defines it, perseverance is "steadfastness in doing something despite difficulty or delay in achieving success." This means that even when we cannot see the light at the end of the tunnel, we need to keep going. Not giving up is key. I believe many people could succeed in life, but they simply don't continue to try. Thomas Edison said, 'Many of life's failures are people who did not realize how close they were to success when they gave up.'

"**Don't stop when the going gets tough.** The big break, the million-dollar deal, the next major company or idea, could be just around the corner, but none of those things will take flight if one gives up too soon. Perseverance requires hard work. It requires a keep-going attitude in the face of adversity. Many people get off to a great start, but the minute they hit a rough patch, they panic and throw in the towel. Life is riddled with setbacks. In fact, disappointment and challenges are almost inevitable. The top athletes in the world know this more than anyone. Many experience major setback when they get injured and must work hard to get themselves back in the game. At times, it can feel easier to just give up. Setbacks can make or break us. Instead of running from adversity, we must figure out how to face — and even embrace — it. Some of the most successful entrepreneurs in the world experienced such tremendous setbacks that they considered giving up and closing their doors. But they did not, and today, they enjoy thriving businesses.

"**Remember Your Calling.** In order to persevere, one must be fueled by their calling. Leonardo Da Vinci said, "Make your work to be in keeping with your purpose." If a CEO or business owner does not believe their work is their calling, they will not keep persevering. Once they embrace that calling and become passionate about it, the sky is the limit. If you are struggling, remember what first inspired you. Take yourself back to your first vision, your first dream for your company or yourself. Perseverance requires effort, hard work, and determination. Leonardo Da Vinci, Steve Jobs, and Thomas Edison all faced criticism and adversity, but they did not give up. As a leader of my company, I hope to follow in their footsteps, embracing the never-give-up mentality that's brought me to success. Perseverance is not only a good idea — it is essential for success. We will fall on hard times and face unwanted challenges. We will feel tempted to give up at times. But when we keep pressing on and remember our roots, we will find the fuel to keep going."

"Christo, that is wonderful advice. It seems like you really work to live The 4 P's of Success. I have always thought of perseverance as a critical skill for any leader, but I think you do a great job of really hammering home the point. I know we have been talking for almost an hour, and I want to be respectful of your time. Would it be ok with you if I followed up via email with any other questions?"

Christo quickly responded: "Of course John. I am at your disposal. I love sharing information and am hopeful some of the insight I provided will help you along the way."

John said, "I am sure that it will. Thank you so much for your time and effort. I learned a great deal from our call and I am excited to share it with my own team. Have a great day Christo. I hope we can chat again soon."

"Ciao, John. Make it a great day."

John hung up the phone with Christo and began to recap their call together. Christo provided enormous insight into such a meaningful concept. He took out his journal and wrote down each of the 4 P's, each followed by a substantial and influential quotation that helped to remind him to remain dedicated to precision, planning, prioritization, and perseverance. He then tore out the piece of paper, and hung it on his wall, right next to his laptop. It read:

Precision

Planning

Prioritization

Perseverance

"Being busy does not always mean real work. The object of all work is production or accomplishment and to either of these ends there must be forethought, system, planning, intelligence, and honest purpose, as well as perspiration. Seeming to do is not doing."
— Thomas Edison

John would be reminded of each of these every day of his life. They were instilled in his own journey, and he remained steadfast in continuing to build a company that stood for these success pillars. The past few months of his business had truly tested the strength of his own success, but he did feel as if his company rebounded, overcoming one large obstacle and poised to handle many others. Only time would tell what the future held, but John decided to focus on the controllables, breathe deeply and often, and concentrate his efforts on building a strong foundation, so when the storms would come, he'd be ready.

CHAPTER 12:

LESSON #12: EXECUTING YOUR ENTREPRENEURIAL GAME PLAN:

Assess, Evaluate, and Deliver

"However beautiful the strategy, you should occasionally look at the results"
— **Sir Winston Churchill**

It had been over two years since John left the comforts of a six-figure job and all the benefits that went along with it. His road to this point in his life was not always a smooth one, and his Telos had seen substantial obstacles over the past year. At one point, they were on the brink of losing a multi-million-dollar client, but through a quick response and a remarkable amount of perseverance, they bounced back. Those were dark times, but John fixed them through a responsive approach where he and his team addressed the problem head-on and refused to hide or run away from it.

But they deployed a team of software technicians to resolve the glitches in their operating programs. Shortly thereafter, Telos implemented a help-desk strategy, where any of their infrastructures using their technology could reach a live customer service representative that could troubleshoot and solve most problems over the phone. Telos also updated their technology to include web conferencing, where a company rep could directly connect with the computer at issue and work towards a resolution. These additional safeguards demonstrated Telos's dedication to their customers and helped them to rebound from catastrophic consequences.

John learned an enormous amount from the difficult times. His team was now better-trained, and John learned to focus more on his blind spots, rather than waiting for tragedy to strike. He also gained valuable insight into the needs of his partners and colleagues, recognizing that failing to plan for the "worst case scenario" was nothing short of a disservice to his clients.

So there he was, a few years after the biggest decision of his life. John reflected upon his journey and enjoyed reading through the journal he created along the way. It offered insight into his darkest moments, as well as his greatest successes. He could literally feel the emotion jumping off the pages, and with each page John was transported back to the defining moments through the life of his business. John exhaled deeply, felt an overwhelming sense of satisfaction, and couldn't believe it was already New Year's Eve. The year had flown by, and while some days were more difficult than others, he made it. He was exactly where he wanted to be and couldn't help but take a moment to pat himself on his back, something he rarely took the time to do.

But that pat was a short-lived one. He knew he had to stay ahead of the curve. The technology sector was a rapidly changing area, and he strived to be a leading force. So John shifted his attention to the future. He wondered what it would hold for Telos? John hoped for steady growth and the continued ability to deliver educational products to those in need of them. He then turned to his newest adventure, a philanthropic spin off of Telos. John wanted to leave an even greater imprint on the world, and Telos started to build small schools in third world countries, providing them with computers and software to expedite the educational process. John decided that he would funnel no less than 10% of the company profits into this endeavor. He started Telos to fulfill his passion to serve others. And he was now in a position to do just that. His success could help others, and he was ready to forge ahead with even greater purpose.

John picked up the phone to call Sri and wish him a Happy New Year. Sri answered after two rings. "Hey John — Happy New Year. How are you?"

"Hey Sri. I am doing great. I just wanted to reach out and wish you a Happy New Year before the evening started. Do you have any big plans?"

"Not so much. We are going to dinner with a few friends and then will likely go and watch the ball drop from the balcony of a nearby high rise in New York. What about you?"

"I don't have any plans. But I decided I'd catch up on some paperwork and then crack open a good bottle of Bordeaux to ring in the New Year with my family."

Sri responded, "That sounds pretty relaxing. I am jealous. So, have you decided on a New Year's resolution?"

John paused.

"I haven't given it a terrible amount of thought. But I have been working hard to kick off a philanthropic opportunity for Telos. I have put the wheels in motion, and we are a certified 501(c)(3). I am excited to give back to the community to take my passion and purpose one step further."

"That is great, John. What a worthwhile and meaningful decision. I am so happy you are headed in that direction. There is absolutely no downside to taking some of your success and using it to help others. What about scaling your business? Have you given that any thought?"

"I have. I want to continue our controlled growth. I don't want to expand too fast, as I know it can create growing pains for a young business. But I feel it necessary to do all I can to invite in meaningful progress. I have this idea...it is called an entrepreneurial game plan. Just like every great sports team has an executable playbook, I think every company should have the same. So I decided I would begin to develop the idea and actually work to write a book on the topic. My hope is that the next year gives me the opportunity to blow out this charitable endeavor and complete a book on how business leaders and executives can form their own entrepreneurial game plans."

Sri jumped in: "John, that sounds awesome. Entrepreneurs need to have a definitive and written game plan outlining their business model. You should chat with my friend, Edouard Sterngold, who goes by Ed. He has a pretty cool story. In 2004, he started a business called Bevyz. For a long time, he was an international businessman in the beverage industry, but saw a larger prospect in front of him. So he left it all behind, took a risk, and is now doing extremely well. In fact, in December of 2014, Keurig Green Mountain, Inc. (Keurig) acquired Bevyz for approximately $270 million. Let me CC you on an email to him. I would bet he'd be willing and happy to offer you some great advice that you could incorporate into your entrepreneurial game plan. Happy New Year, my friend — make it the best one yet."

"Thanks Sri. Happy New Year to you, too. I am so thankful for all you have done for me. This is going to be a great year."

Even after two years, John still was in awe of the great generosity people offered to him. Just like all those that came before, Ed was more than willing to jump on a call and share his knowledge and experience with John. He responded a couple of days after Sri's initial email, immediately apologizing for the delay. John exchanged a couple of emails with him, and they agreed to hop on a Skype call at noon.

John was extremely excited for the call. Since starting Telos, John knew the greatest business assets he had were his connections and his mentors. Professionally, no singular facet of his life provided superior value. Sri was kind enough to introduce John to his friends and John made the most of those contacts. He never overstepped his boundaries, but certainly took advantage of the time these experts were willing to offer. As John did some quick tallies, he realized this would be the twelfth mentor to whom he spoke.

John looked at his clock and realized it was just a few minutes before noon. He opened his laptop, logged on, and clicked on the Skype application. After entering his username and password, the app powered to life, and he saw an incoming friend request from Ed. He clicked on it, and it began to connect with Ed. Moments later, the window went live, and he saw a video image of Ed on his computer screen.

"Ed, how are you? Happy New Year! Thanks so much for connecting with me. Sri spoke very highly of you. I am so glad you could find some extra time in your schedule. This is truly an honor. Sri didn't hesitate in recommending I speak with you. We were discussing the future of my business and my New Year's resolution, and he thought I could benefit greatly from your journey."

John watched on as Ed smiled, shifted back into his oversized leather chair, and said: "Thanks John. Sri is too kind. I wouldn't expect anything less from him. He is a dear friend, and I am always more than willing to connect and see what information I can share."

"Wonderful. I am so excited to learn more about you. I did a little bit of independent research, but would you be willing to share a little bit more information about you and your company."

"No problem. I founded Bevyz in 2004 after having thought about it for many years. I did it based on my understanding of the industry and the long-term consumer trends I identified. I discussed my concept with a few people whose input I trusted. I then forged ahead based on my intuition.

"Bevyz is a beverage company that actually combines the drink and the technology to deliver it. Bevyz is an extraordinary company with a unique opportunity to shake-up the global beverage industry. We have the only innovative multi-drink system in the world, which dispenses incredible-tasting hot, cold, and sparkling drinks on your kitchen countertop. In the coming months, together with our partner Cuisinart, we will be bringing our groundbreaking multi-drink system to the US consumer market, with the launch of our new Fresh machine.

"It is an exciting opportunity. Our management team has an awesome track record in creating great-tasting drinks and beverage systems. The aim with Bevyz is to continuously make our consumers' drink experience refreshing — by creating innovative, yet easy-to-use, single-serve capsule systems that make a limitless variety of premium beverages. We have created an unrivalled network of world-renowned engineering and ingredients companies to make this happen.

"Bevyz is derived from various historic words, including "bevy" from the Middle English, meaning a large group or collection. Also, the Old French "beivre" and the Latin "bibere" meaning "to drink.""

With that said, I think you'd find helpful the four steps I took to turn the idea behind Bevyz into a successful reality. These include:

1. Assembling a multidisciplinary team to evaluate the concepts and come up with possible solutions of how this innovative concept could best work in real life.
2. Developing the building stones of the business (i.e. the vision, mission, the strategy, and business plan) while executing it by setting up the business in the most efficient way and assembling a star team.
3. Fundraising in repeated rounds while growing the business and balancing short-, mid-, and long-term interests.
4. Positioning the business as an innovative technology company; building an ecosystem with leading global companies in the appliance and beverage industry to assure a winning exit strategy.

"I eventually sold the company with successful results for shareholders, employees, and other stakeholders. Fundamentally, those were always in the cards for any company I built. I know that was probably more information than you would need, but I am extremely proud of our company and its deliverables."

"No—thank you for sharing. That is extremely impressive. Tell me a little bit about your management style. I guess you could call it the 'execution' side of things."

"No problem. I ensure we clearly formulate our vision, mission, values and strategy. We then collectively work to see it through and ensure they are widely and repeatedly communicated and understood. We take all efforts to connect our actions to our thoughts. When we discover an inconsistency in implementation, we strive to swiftly correct it. We also celebrate success publicly and frequently.

"Especially when it comes to business, the plan will never exactly unfold as anticipated. Set up a solid but adaptable framework and instill a mindset with open-minded and flexible people to adjust to changing circumstances. Without a compass, you can't navigate and reach your goals."

"Vision without execution is hallucination."
— **Thomas Edison**

"I feel that strategic execution starts with the culture of accountability, prioritization, and timely decision-making on key strategic and operational initiatives. Successful execution comes with clearly defined roles and decision-making rights that are aligned with a proper compensation structure to motivate people to act in the best interest of the organization, rather in their own individual interest, and well-defined communication channels that feed required information in a timely manner. But, at the end of the day, just like in sports, great leaders have great game plans, anticipating, inspiring, and delivering."

John smiled widely, and thanked Ed for everything.

"You bet. No problem. As we were chatting, I pulled up some old reference articles I enjoy reading. I am emailing them to you now. Talk to you soon, John."

Shortly after John logged off the Skype call, a window appeared on his screen, signaling new mail. It came from Ed. As he opened the email, he saw a number of attachments. He downloaded each one and began reading. The first attachment was an article written by Phillipe

Lafortune and entitled *Execution Leadership: The Art of Getting Things Done.*[6] He started to read:

The New CEO: Chief 'Execution' Officer

Execution is an art; an art that separates successful organizations from less successful ones. As such, Execution is one of a leader's most important job. Period.

A brilliant strategy, blockbuster product, or breakthrough technology can put you on the competitive map, but only solid execution can keep you there. You have to be able to deliver on your intent.

*Execution is the biggest challenge or issue facing organizations today. At its core, it is a culture with a specific set of behaviors, processes and techniques; more than anything, it is a disciplined and systematic approach to planning, implementation, and progress assessment. Execution is not just something that does or doesn't get done; it is not just a tactic, and it is not something to be delegated. Execution should be a central part of a company's strategy and goals and the most important job of any leader. An execution culture is composed of three core processes of any business together to get things done on time: **the people process**, **the strategy**, and **the operating plan**.*

Execution is the result of thousands of decisions made every day by employees acting according to the information they have and their own self-interest. In our line of work, helping companies to execute more effectively, there are four fundamental building blocks executives can use to influence those actions: clarifying decision rights, designing

6   https://www.linkedin.com/pulse/chief-execution-officer-philippe-lafortune

information flows, aligning motivators, and making changes to structure.

There are many business leaders today that still think of Execution as the tactical side of business — something which they delegate while they indulge themselves in the perceived "bigger" topics. Consequently, they do not comprehend that Execution is not just tactics — it is a discipline and a system of its own. It has to be ingrained into an organization's objectives, culture, structure, and processes. The leader himself must be the <u>Master of Execution</u>. This is both true in big and in small companies.

John pondered what he just read for a few minutes. He then continued on.

How to become Master of Execution

In their excellent book entitled <u>Execution: The Disciple of Getting Things Done</u>, Larry Bossidy and Ram Charan list the following three building blocks that need to be in place in order to make Execution happen in your organization.

*Building Block One: **The Leader's Seven Essential Behaviors***

To install and to keep up the real spirit, concept, and processes of Execution — and to avoid becoming a micro-manager — there are seven essential behaviors which characterize a leader of execution:

- *Know your people and your business: Be engaged with your business, live your business, and be where the action is.*

- *Insist on realism: It's the heart of execution. Start by being realistic yourself. Then you make sure realism is the goal of all dialogues in the organization.*
- *Set clear goals and priorities: Focus on three — four clear priorities that everyone can grasp. Speak and act simply and directly.*
- *Follow through: Lack of it is a major cause of poor execution. Implement detailed action plans and make specific people accountable for results.*
- *Reward the doers: If you want people to produce specific results, you need to reward them accordingly. Either in base pay or in bonuses and stock options.*
- *Expand people's capabilities through coaching: Pass on your knowledge, wisdom, and experience to the next generation of leaders. Every encounter is an opportunity to coach.*
- *Know yourself: It takes emotional fortitude to be open to whatever information you need, whether it's what you like to hear or not.*

Building Block Two: **Creating The Framework For Cultural Change**

Most efforts at cultural change fail because they are not linked to improving the business outcomes. The ideas and tools of cultural change are fuzzy and disconnected from strategic and operational realities. To change a business's culture, you need a set of processes — social operating mechanisms — that will change the beliefs and behavior of people in ways that are directly linked to bottom-line results.

The basic premise is simple: Cultural change gets real when your aim is execution. You don't need a lot of complex theory or employee surveys to use this framework. You need to change people's behavior so that they produce results. First, you need to explain to people what results you're looking for. Then, you discuss how to get those results, as a key element of the coaching process. Then, you reward people for delivering the results. If they come up short, you provide additional training and coaching, possibly withdraw rewards, look for other tasks and/or jobs for them, or even let them go, if it were the best option for all main stakeholders. When you do these things correctly and sincerely, you create a culture of getting things done.

Building Block Three: **The Job No Leader Should Delegate—Having the Right People in the Right Place.**

An organization's human beings are its most reliable resource for generating excellent results year after year. Their judgments, experiences, and capabilities make the difference between success and failure. Sounds familiar? Yet the same leaders who exclaim that "people are our most important asset" usually do not think very hard about choosing the right people for the right jobs. They either do not have precise ideas about what the jobs require (not only today, but tomorrow) or they're too busy thinking about how to make their companies bigger. What they're overlooking is that the quality of their people is the best competitive differentiator.

Often leaders may not know enough about the people they're appointing. They may also pick people with whom they're comfortable, rather than others who have better skills for the job. They may not have the courage to discriminate between strong and weak performers and take the necessary actions. All of these reflect one absolutely fundamental shortcoming: The leaders aren't personally committed to the people process and deeply engaged in it. However, it's a job you have to love doing as a leader.

John sat back and thought about the article. He wholeheartedly agreed with its message. John thought this to be brilliant. It was right in synch with his notion of an Entrepreneurial Game Plan . He closed his laptop and took out his journal, feeling inspired and determined to put together his Entrepreneurial Game Plan. He wrote in big bolded letters the words:

The Entrepreneurial Game Plan

"A good plan violently executed now is better than a perfect plan executed next week."
— **George Patton**

Under those words, John wrote the following: John decided to put together a simplified Entrepreneurial Game Plan based on Ed's and all other advisors' teachings over the last two years, on how to successfully formulate, execute, and communicate the strategy across the organization in aligning towards achieving organizational goals and objectives. John finally felt he was able to put together a one-page Entrepreneurial Game Plan. He would share this with each and every team member in his organization to ensure that he is aligned across the board. It looked like this:

Entrepreneurial Game Plan

John was pleased with what he saw. He decided he would take this document and frame it, leaving it on his desk and in direct sight. John shared it with the team, hoping it would eventually become their own operating framework, so they could create their own Game Plan within the company, while also working to play an integral role in the development of the team and the company's overall goals. Telos had a bright future — one that would almost certainly offer John enormous success and a fantastic opportunity to make a difference in the world. To John, there was nothing more important than education. In fact, it was his own educational journey that motivated the drastic steps he took just a few years ago. If he could offer the world the same sort of journey, he knew he'd done a good job.

BUILDING FOR THE FUTURE

J ohn awoke to feel the warmth of the sun dancing into his small cottage. He lifted his head from the pillow, and grabbed his pants and long-sleeved shirt. He put them on, brushed his teeth, and located his socks and shoes. John flipped over his shoes, and forcibly struck the bottom of them. When he arrived in Africa, Frank, his tour guide, told him to always double check his shoes for snakes and spiders. Frightening at first, John had gotten used to it over the past few weeks. He recognized that it was better than the alternative. John confirmed no creepy crawlers made their home in the warm shoes, and placed them on his feet, lacing them tight.

This day would be special. Over the past three years, Telos worked hard to offer educational opportunities to third world countries. Telos provided software and computers to underprivileged communities. Most of these "students" had never been in a formal classroom, and some never even opened a book. Their ages ranged from five —15, and many did not know how to count or even read.

Sadly, they were lucky if they found themselves with a full stomach of food each day.

But through his philanthropic organization, Telos Teaches, John was ready to take things one step further. John had flown to Africa to open his first school. He had made the 20-hour flight a few weeks ago and appreciated the opportunity to get to know the community. He toured Africa, and learned an enormous amount about African culture and the challenges the country faced. In the last week, John had enjoyed the chance to actually complete the finishing touches on the school. He installed the computers, software, and even pitched in to affix the beautiful Telos Teaches sign to the front of the wooden double doors. It was an uplifting experience to hammer in the final nails.

And so, John opened the door to his cottage, walked outside, and felt the strenuous heat overtake his senses. He immediately started to sweat, still not used to the 100+ degree heat and humidity that Africa enjoyed during the summer season. He made his way through the small village he stayed in, and in the direction of the Telos Teaches school. As he arrived, he saw a large crowd forming in front of the school. Villagers, new students, and the executive board from Telos greeted him. John saw Frank headed in his direction, and they embraced with a big hug and handshake.

"Today is the big day," Frank cheerfully said.

"I know. I cannot believe it. I feel like I have been waiting for this day for my entire life. I am just so proud that, together, we could offer these students an opportunity at education. No child should be without the basic learning tools, and we are providing them with an enormous chance to not only learn, but to teach others. This is a special day."

"Thank you my friend. The village could not be more appreciative. This is just the beginning."

Frank ushered John to the front of the school where he was surrounded by colleagues, friends, and loved ones. In front of him was a bright red ribbon, held by two of the first students that would enroll in the school. Behind John were the other twenty-three students that would comprise the inaugural class. They were bookended by a teacher on each side of them. The leader of the small village stood up, offering words of encouragement and thanking John for all of his work.

Frank then gave John the scissors, and with a warm heart and purposeful soul, John cut the big red ribbon. Telos Teaches was open for business.

ABOUT THE AUTHOR

SRI GADDAM

Srikanth Gaddam is a seasoned entrepreneur who has launched four successful companies in the last 14 years, including ERP Analysts, Inc. Mr. Gaddam attended the Owner/President/Management program (OPM 43) offered by the Harvard Business School. He earned an MBA degree from the Max M. Fisher College of Business.  He was a **Business First "Forty under 40" honoree and 2015 "Entrepreneurship and Innovation Award"** recipient from Fisher College of Business.

He serves as President and CEO of ERP Analysts, a company that provides Oracle, Business Intelligence and Big Data consulting services, and delivers successful projects to mid-market and Fortune 500 firms. He helped the company expand from a two-person organization in **2003 to a 75 million-dollar company** serving clients in 36 states and the Caribbean.

Under his leadership, ERP Analysts, Inc. has been recognized by Inc. as one of the 5,000 fastest growing companies for seven consecutive years. The firm was a part of Deloitte's Fast 500 and Columbus Business First's Fast 50 lists. Additionally, ERP Analysts has been honored with **"101 National Best and Brightest Companies to Work For"** and "Business First **"#1 Best Places to Work in Central Ohio"** in 2015.

Mr. Gaddam founded "Sponsor Kids Foundation," an NGO that supports and makes a positive impact in the lives of 100 impoverished children around the world. Mr. Gaddam co-authored a book, "Roadmap to Success," with Deepak Chopra, Ken Blanchard and other entrepreneurial leaders for strategies for success.

Morgan James
Speakers Group

➤ www.TheMorganJamesSpeakersGroup.com

We connect Morgan James published
authors with live and online events
and audiences whom will benefit
from their expertise.

Morgan James makes all of our titles available
through the Library for All Charity Organization.

www.LibraryForAll.org